Not Your Mother's Book . . .

On Being a Stupid Kid

Created by
Dahlynn McKowen,
Ken McKowen and Laurel McHargue

Enjoy!
Leadville Laurel

Published by
Publishing Syndicate

PO Box 607
Orangevale California 95662
www.PublishingSyndicate.com

Not Your Mother's Book . . .
On Being a Stupid Kid

*We would like to thank the many individuals
who granted us permission to reprint their stories.
See the complete listing beginning on page 302.*

Created and edited by Dahlynn McKowen,
Ken McKowen and Laurel McHargue

Cover and book design by Publishing Syndicate
Cover photo: llike/Shutterstock.com
Copyeditor: Terri Elders

Published by
Publishing Syndicate
PO Box 607
Orangevale California 95662

www.PublishingSyndicate.com
www.Facebook.com/PublishingSyndicate
Twitter: @PublishingSynd

Print Edition ISBN: 978-1-938778-02-5
EPUB Digital Edition ISBN: 978-1-938778-03-2
Library of Congress Control Number 2012916847

Printed in Canada

This book is a collaborative effort. Writers from all over the world submitted their work for consideration, with 59 stories making the final cut. All contributors are compensated for their stories and are invited to take part in a media campaign.

Publishing Syndicate strongly encourages you to submit your story to one of its many anthologies. You'll find information on how to do so at the end of this book, starting on page 304.

To my parents,
Patricia and Charles Bernier,
proud progenitors of five perfect princesses,
and to my sisters—
Christine, Susan, Charlene and Carol—
who didn't *always* snitch.
~~ Laurel McHargue

Laurel with her dad and mom

From left: Charlene, Susan, Laurel, Carol,
Patricia (Sexy Momma!) and Christine

CONTENTS

Acknowledgments

Lots of people to thank, all around!

Our families:
Thank you to Laurel's parents for believing in her ever since she was a chubby, little freckle-faced kid.

Thank you to Laurel's husband, Mike, for saying, "Sure! Take a year off! Follow your dream!" And, in her words, "for so much more."

Thank you to Laurel's sons, Nick and Jake, for laughing at her stories and for making her laugh whenever they're together.

Thank you to Dahlynn's teen son Shawn, for putting up with the general craziness that yet another new book has brought to the McKowen household.

And our extended family:
Thank you, Terri Elders, for your splendid copyedit expertise. You keep the production wheels humming and us on the straight and narrow!

Thank you, Paul Krupin, for overseeing our media and public relations campaign. Through your company Direct Contact PR (www.DirectContactPR.com), you have never let us down, helping us navigate the world of promotion and making our books shine!

Thank you, Pat Nelson, for being the proofreader of proofreaders. You outdid yourself!

Thank you, Maggie Lamond Simone, for introducing Laurel to the McKowens. This book wouldn't be here without that introduction.

Thank you, Ed Quillen and Michael Rosso, former and current editors of *Colorado Central Magazine*, for publishing Laurel's earlier stories and encouraging her students to submit their stories. Your magazine provided Laurel her first professional writing platform!

Thank you, NYMB co-creators, for joining us on this amazing journey. And Laurel adds a special thanks for the encouragement and offers of assistance in creating her very first NYMB title.

Most of all, thank you to those who have graciously shared their stories with us, even though they were all pretty stupid. We couldn't have done it without you!

~~ Dahlynn McKowen, Ken McKowen and Laurel McHargue

Introduction

Stupidity is better kept a secret than displayed.
~~ Heraclitus (c. 535 – c. 475 B.C.)

—or—

Stupid is as stupid does.
~~ Forrest Gump, quoting his momma

Two memorable quotes by two noteworthy people.

Ancient Greek philosopher Heraclitus was clearly one of the more advanced thinkers of his time. His teachings have been eternalized on papyrus scrolls—the ancient version of today's computer hard drives—and students of philosophy around the globe continue to study him. But did he truly believe that stupidity should remain hidden? We will never really know.

On the other hand, Forrest Gump shares a modern-day version of Greek philosophy. This legendary fictional character, created by author Winston Groom in his book by the same name and brought to life on the big screen by actor Tom Hanks, says it like it is. Plain and simple: you are what you do!

Many might argue we live in a time that honors buffoonery, and the flood of television shows, movies and Internet posts presenting perilous stunts and bad behavior just might prove that point. I can only imagine what Heraclitus and Forrest would say if they were sitting together today watching an episode of *Jackass*:

"Hark, my young Gump, what sayeth thou of such

preposterous and illogical endeavors, of such foolish mirth makers? Are they mad?"

"Momma'd call 'em stupid. Would you like to share my chocolates?"

It's nice to think that people of every generation have been able to enjoy stress-releasing guffaws at the expense of those who willingly offer their slapstick escapades and silly stories, as many have for this book. When the call went out to "tell the world about something stupid you did as a kid," we had no idea what to expect. The response was tremendous! Stories came from across the generational spectrum from both men and women, and making the final selections was difficult; there were so many crazy accounts from which to choose!

We all are human. We've all made stupid decisions in our past, and if we somehow managed to remain alive despite ourselves, maybe we owe it to others to display our humanity—sorry, Heraclitus!—rather than hide it. They say laughter is the best medicine, and the stories in this anthology prove it. They will bring a smile to your face and make you think back to your own misadventures.

Back to our two philosophers. Perhaps the company he kept led Heraclitus to the conclusion that "many do not understand such things as they encounter, nor do they learn by their experience, but they think they do." As for Forrest, the lessons he learned from his unusual experiences led him to greatness, and not one among us will ever forget the message that lives on today, that life is like a box of chocolates—mixed nuts and all.

~~ Laurel McHargue

CHAPTER ONE

Double-Dog Dare

Those "look-at-me!" moments that
NO ONE will ever forget!

Vaya con Dios, Baby!

by

John J. Lesjack

Every winter, somewhere in Minnesota, an old car is placed on a frozen lake. Rotary Club members take bets on the exact day and time in the spring after the ice thaws when the car will sink to the bottom of the lake. I don't know if that's a true story or not, but it reminds me of my unique experience with a frozen lake, an old car and some friends in February 1953—and mine IS a true story.

We were all high school students between part-time jobs, not involved in any sport, and hanging out at the typical malt shop, which in this case was Rexall's Pharmacy in East Detroit, Michigan. We had all developed the same affliction that Saturday: Too much time on our hands, too much cabin fever. Names in this story have been withheld to protect everyone involved, including their children and grandchildren.

In post WWII days, just cruising with your friends was an

adventure where five guys in one car would try to pick up five girls in another car. In all my years, I never heard of this system succeeding, and today I wonder where they would have put the five girls, had five been picked up. But on that bitterly cold Saturday, all teenage girls in our town had the good sense to stay home.

My four buddies and I showed no such sense and departed Rexall's with no particular destination in mind. In school we had been taught, "Don't borrow trouble," but Shakespeare was wasted on us. Because I had no chains on my tires, and the roads were clear all the way to Metropolitan Beach on the shores of Lake St. Clair, that's where we went.

The lake was 26 miles long and 24 miles wide. Canada was across the water from us even though overcast skies prevented us from seeing it as we sat in my green 1937 Chevrolet on the frozen wasteland. Maybe we looked like Hannibal before he crossed the Alps, or Caesar before he conquered the known world, or General Patton before he . . . you get the picture, right? Who knows why five teenage boys do anything? Maybe the Italian in our group said, "Veni, vidi, vici." I came, I saw, I conquered . . . Lake St. Clair.

Before us lay the lake, frozen as usual this time of the year, and abandoned by all forms of life. No ice skaters, no ice boats, no ice shanties. We had the entire lake to ourselves—which should have told us something—but winter sometimes numbs the brains of teenage boys. This was one of those days.

"Let's go to Canada," one guy said.

"Not enough gas," I said.

"Let's get something to eat," another one said.

"No money," we all said.

"I dare you to spin some doughnuts," said yet another friend.

"Yeah, do it!" cried another inspirational voice. The idea resonated with all of us. The dare was on, and five teenage boys were transformed from loafers in a malt shop to young men with a purpose in life.

I downshifted, let out the clutch and drove slowly over the frozen sand onto the ice. This was my first year of driving and I spun my tires. What did you expect? I was only 17 and had recently purchased the car because the radio worked. Hey, what's a car without a good radio? A teenager has to hear songs from the *Hit Parade*. In fact, Kay Starr was singing *Wheel of Fortune* as we headed out to our destiny.

I drove slowly and built up momentum. The car was doing 5, 10, 15 mph and more, and that unleashed a discussion from the unlicensed people in the back seat, none of whom had experience in spinning doughnuts on Lake St. Clair, but who had suddenly become experts on ice driving.

"Slam on the brakes and see what happens!"

"No, turn the steering wheel as far as it goes first!"

"No, stupid, turn off the engine and let it lock up."

When my car reached what I felt was critical mass, I slammed on the brakes AND turned the steering wheel. Remember, in those days seat belts were unknown, and everyone in the car was thrown in a heap to one side. Traveling on ice at 25 mph in frigid weather, the car spun round and round. Talk about a thrill! Rides at nearby Jefferson Beach Amusement Park had nothing on us! The sensation was exhilarating! Who said youth was wasted on the young? The young knew how to have a good time! We laughed until we were exhausted, but more importantly, no one threw up.

Spinning doughnuts in right turns and then left turns took us farther and farther out on the ice. We were laughing and enjoying being teenagers, listening to our music on the radio and contributing nothing to the gross national product except good feelings. What great memories we were building, all the while supported by some ice above lots of cold water on an overcast day.

My car's heater kept us plenty warm until the guy riding shotgun decided to roll down his window and let in some fresh air. That was when we all heard a loud, prolonged crack.

"Sounds like thunder," the first guy said. He switched off the radio.

"That's not thunder. That's the ice cracking!" someone said from the back seat. Those guys were like a Greek chorus.

"Oh, my God, we're all going to die!" one weenie yelled.

"Ice is still solid," I said, "But I'm heading back to shore, just in case." I had paid $175 for that car. Why let it sink in the lake? Only where was shore? All we could see was ice and a dark, ominous sky. Oh, shit! We had lost sight of land.

"We'll never make it! I'm getting out!"

"Shut up and sit down. I'm not opening the door at this speed."

Like a miracle, the sun broke through, which solved one problem—we could see the shoreline. As we approached land all we could see was a narrow slit of fresh water between the ice and the beach. Shallow water meant thin ice. How shallow? How thin?

We didn't have much time with the ice cracking underneath us and the sun warming everything above. "I'm going for it," I said. I pulled out the throttle, kept that little car in first gear and traveled faster and faster.

"We won't run out of gas, will we?" one guy asked.

"Are you crazy? We'll all sink like rocks first!" someone shouted. Then all we heard was the sound of the 4-cylinder engine and we hoped that this was the little engine that could.

We hit the open water and the front wheels dropped down with a bang, but the rear wheels and low gear and our momentum—and the dead weight in the back seat—propelled us through the ice and shallow water! The rear tires dug into the frozen sand and soon we were safe in the paved parking lot where we yelled and laughed! One guy burst into tears! Another guy said, "Let's do it again!" We nearly threw him out of the car.

Once on the main road, I turned the radio on and heard *Vaya con Dios*, by Les Paul and Mary Ford. How appropriate! "Vaya con dios, baby," I said to Metro Beach and headed for the malt shop where we told our little drama all afternoon. Ironically, we'd made stupid decisions before and we were soooo lucky today, but we acted like heroes because we had cheated death. Maybe youth *is* wasted on the young.

Betters in Minnesota put their money down to see if they could profit from their old car sinking in the lake. My friends and I bet on ourselves and won. That's the kind of profit I like! But it's a lesson that is rarely easy and never beautiful—except in retrospect.

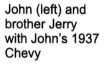

John (left) and brother Jerry with John's 1937 Chevy

Wile E. Coyote and Me

by
Pamela Frost

"Wile E. Coyote, Genius"—like me. He was my child-hood hero. No wait, he's still my hero. As a child I made a business card, "Pamela K. Frost, Genius," just like his. Being a genius is not easy, as demonstrated by my idol. Even though the rest of his card read "Have brain, will travel," gravity foiled his plans over and over again.

In 1964, I was eight years old and living in Cleveland, Ohio. I was well on my way to establishing genius status, especially in the eyes of my four-year-old brother Hollis. He followed me everywhere.

This was a time before zillions of television channels and millions of video games. We were not glued to electronic devices; we were left to discover our world and invent our own fun. Being city kids, our world encompassed only one block, since we weren't allowed to cross the street. Inevitably, along about August, summertime fun of playing house and riding our bikes failed to thrill. Even roller derby competitions in the garage became boring.

One day, during yet another game of hide-and-seek, I discovered I could climb up onto the garage roof using an old metal trash can with a milk crate stacked on top. Once up top, I squatted on the hot roof, holding my hand over my mouth to keep from giggling as everyone searched for me for a long time.

Finally, my best friend, Mary, yelled, "Ali, ali oxen free."

I jumped up and shouted, "Looky here!"

My three friends and little brother gazed up in amazement. "How'd you get up there?"

James and Mary were tall, like me, and had no trouble climbing up onto the roof. But we had to grab Hollis by the hands and haul him up. The same with Mary's little sister Cindy. After we admired the view, there wasn't much left to do up there. When we went to climb down, we saw that the milk crate had slid off the trash can, which must have fallen with Cindy's ascent.

I couldn't yell for my mother—if she knew I was on the garage roof with my little brother, a whooping was certainly in my future. So I eased my body over the edge and hung by my fingertips for a few moments before dropping safely to the soft grass behind the garage. My heart raced with excitement.

While retrieving the crate to rescue the others, I heard James say, "Go on, Mary. You do it."

Mary took hesitant baby steps to the edge of the roof.

"Come on, I dare you," her brother said.

Chewing a fingernail, Mary sat down on the edge, her legs dangling.

James taunted, "I double-dog dare you."

She gave him the look of death as she eased her long lanky frame over the edge and dropped. Her feet slipped and she landed flat on her butt. The others on the roof howled with laughter. I rushed to help her up.

Mary stood up, unharmed, dusted herself off and yelled to James, "Come on, your turn! You chicken or something?"

He stared, open-mouthed.

Mary began dancing around the yard, flapping make-believe chicken wings and squawking. I joined in.

James walked to the edge of the roof, paused and leaped off, landing with a gymnastic tumble.

Not to be outdone, Mary and I scrambled back up to the roof. I got a running start and went flying off the back of the garage. I felt like Wile E. Coyote hanging in midair for a moment before I landed. We pretended we were competing in the Olympics, and Cindy and Hollis were our Olympic judges. The three of us continued to try to outdo each other for the best style and longest leap. My adrenaline surged.

I was on the roof, catching my breath, when I saw a huge Sears delivery truck coming slowly down our street. "Look!" I shouted. "Somebody's getting something new!"

Mary said excitedly, "That's our new refrigerator!"

James' eyes lit up, "Do you think it'll come in a box?"

We helped the little ones down off the roof and ran to the sidewalk just as the big burly delivery men opened the back of the truck to reveal the most amazing box ever.

I asked one of the men, "Hey, mister, can we have the box?"

He chuckled. "Of course you can, if it's all right with your mother."

Mary ran to the house shouting, "Mom! Mom! Can we have the box?"

Her mom came to the door. "What's all the shouting about?"

Mary gasped, "The refrigerator is here. Can we have the box?"

"Sure, honey, I see no harm."

Immediately we began to argue. Cindy said, "Let's make a doll house."

James loudly proclaimed, "It's going to be a spaceship."

Mary said, even louder, "It's my box and it's going to be a boat. We can get old sheets from my mom and make sails."

Somehow, in our young brains, we thought more volume equaled being more right. I was louder still, "A plane. It's got to be a plane!"

My little brother jumped up and down, repeatedly shouting, "We're going to build a plane!"

The others grumbled, but I stood firm. "Majority rules. We're building a plane."

I barked out orders as we drug the box to the backyard, because it was common knowledge that as the neighborhood genius, I was in charge. Cindy and Hollis carried the side of the box which the movers had cut off to get the refrigerator out. Everyone hurried back to their houses to collect supplies and before long, the yard was littered with crayons, tape and construction paper.

We stood back and proudly admired our creation. Mary had drawn a propeller on the nose. Hollis and Cindy had taped black construction paper down the sides for windows. I drew the gauges and dials inside the cockpit. James drew guns on the sheet of cardboard that became the wings and declared it was a fighter plane. We duct-taped the wings across the box.

James was the first to jump in. "I'm the pilot." He made shooting sounds. "Take that, you dirty Russians."

Mary pushed him, "It's my turn. I should go first. It's my box."

He made a growling-dog sound and crawled out of the cockpit.

She sat up straight, took the imaginary wheel and announced in her best I'm-all-grown-up voice, "Good afternoon, ladies and gentlemen, I'm your captain today and we are going to Florida. Fasten your seat belts, please." The rest of us ran around the yard with our arms outstretched, flying our own imaginary planes.

I walked up to Mary and put my hands on my hips and said, "Come on—it's my turn."

She sighed and got out of the plane, but just as I was about to get in, I had a genius thought. "Let's take it up on the roof. Then we can *really* fly."

Simultaneously, Mary said, "Are you crazy?" and James said, "Great idea!"

James began dragging the plane to the back of the garage. "Pam, go up first and I'll push it up, and you grab it."

I did what he said. We struggled, but finally got the box onto the roof. Everyone else climbed up behind it.

James announced, "I'll go first."

Mary grabbed him by the back of the shirt and shouted, "No!"

I said, "She's right. We should have a test flight first."

We got behind the box and pushed it off the roof. It sailed

to the ground and we all cheered. We repeated the difficult process of getting it back up onto the roof.

We got it lined up for the next flight and my little brother jumped in and shouted, "Push me!"

James objected. "It's my turn."

I said, "Don't be such a baby. Let him have a turn. You already got a turn." He pouted, but helped me launch the box off the roof with my little brother inside.

Everything happened so fast. The plane crashed to the ground, the box split apart and my brother landed like a rag doll. He didn't move.

My heart stopped. "Oh, no—I've killed my brother!"

James and I jumped to the ground on each side of the plane. Mary remained frozen on the roof and grabbed Cindy's hand so she wouldn't fall off. Hollis' eyes were bugged out and he was gasping like a catfish out of water.

I said, "That's it, little guy, breathe." James and I pulled him to his feet. We supported him as we all three walked around the yard. I said what the coach had said to me when I fell: "Walk it off. Come on, walk it off."

James joined the chant, "Yeah, you can do it. Walk it off. Be a man."

Hollis continued to gasp. I knew all too well what he was feeling since I loved to swing on the clothesline and it had snapped more than once, leaving me breathless. But still I feared he had broken something. I ran my hands over his body. "Are you OK?" Tears streamed down my face.

He pushed my hands away and managed to say between gasps, "Quit touching me."

I breathed a sigh of relief.

Hollis then staggered toward the house on unsteady legs, simply saying, "I'm telling."

I ran and dropped to my knees in front of him. I took him by the shoulders and looked into his eyes, hoping I could make him see reason. "Oh, please. I beg you. Don't tell Mom. We'll both be grounded—FOREVER!"

He looked unconvinced and tried to push me away.

"Please, I'll do anything."

His eyes sparkled. "Anything?"

"Anything."

He didn't think long. "I want your new transistor radio."

Eagerly I said, "You got it."

"And be my slave for a week. You have to do whatever I say."

"For crying out loud," I protested.

He folded his arms across his chest and gave me that look—he wasn't going to negotiate.

I agreed. "Deal."

Just like Wile E. Coyote, gravity had done me in.

Pam, standing below the infamous garage roof

Roller-Coaster Bra

by
Glady Martin

I was 19 years old when our whole family visited Canada's famous Pacific National Exhibition (PNE) in Vancouver, British Columbia. This was our second trip to PNE; the first had been three years earlier.

On that first trip, my two older cousins—both big burly guys—talked me into getting onto a ride by the name of "The Spider." It was painted shiny black with blinking yellow lights and each leg had a bucket seat that would hold three people. We got into the seat and I figured I would be pretty safe sandwiched between my two cousins. I was wrong! The ride began slowly and quickened its pace, spinning and dipping me into unbelievable dizziness. It was not a fun ride. I vowed silently to myself that I would never attend the PNE again so I wouldn't be subjected to riding any more rides like that one.

Now, less than five years later, I was back at PNE. And,

once again, I became the victim of another scream machine. But this one was far worse and it made The Spider look like a child's teacup ride.

I got sweet-talked into going on the roller coaster!

"It's nothin', Glad. It's like a baby ride," said my mischievous 16-year-old brother Randy.

I thought long and hard before I answered. "Well, OK, Rand . . . if you say so, then I'll go. I trust you because you know how sensitive I am."

I slid into the coaster's car right beside my younger brother and quickly noticed his little grin, the one he got when he knew something really great was about to happen. My stomach fluttered. *What did I get myself into?!* I screamed inside my head. And I wasn't sure if I was dressed properly for the swift and cold ride; I was wearing a pair of shorts and a deep-scoop T-shirt and my waist-length hair was wild and free. But I had no choice because the car started to move. *It's now or never!*

As we started to climb the first hill, I let loose my first blood-curdling scream! I had forgotten how much I hated heights, but I loved my brother and wanted to do this with him. By the second hill, I had nearly lost my voice! By the third hill, I almost broke the rail bar by holding onto it so tightly! Even through all of this horror, I managed to look over at Randy and witness his sheer pleasure as he screeched with delight and laughed at me.

By the end of the ride, I was a little furious with my brother. "Randy . . . you little . . . " I said to him as the ride came to a stop. I climbed out of my seat and was all fired up to get the heck out of there. My hair was tangled into tight frizzy knots around my face and a ball of hair had formed on the crown of my head. I stomped down the exit ramp with nostrils flaring like a raging bull. I had been had—again! *Some baby ride, Randy!*

I cringed to myself about what others thought of me while they waited their turn to ride on this silver, snake-like structure of high speed and curves that a body isn't meant to endure. I was expecting everyone to have a good laugh at my expense because of my reaction and my hair. Not so. I marched past the line of waiting people and they all looked at me with worry on their faces and fear in their eyes. When I got to my family members—who were all laughing—I marched right past them and into the washroom. I looked into the mirror and not only was shocked at the style of my roller-coaster hairdo, but also saw that my bra had slipped up over my boobs and sat on my neck in the open area of my deep-scooped T-shirt!

Yes, my tiny bra did more than go over rollercoaster bumps that day. I stayed in the washroom for a long while before I could come out again. And I did return to the PNE years later with my own little family, but while my husband took the kids on the rides, I stuck close to the animal shows and food building.

My only ride that day was watching others ride—I saw a performance by the Royal Canadian Mounted Police and their regal horses. Decked out in their full red-serge regalia, including shiny riding boots and wide riding hats, the 50 or so riders gracefully directed their mounts to perform for the crowd. The show was set to patriotic music and it was a truly grand sight to witness riders and horses, dancing as one, gracefully completing assorted angles, circles and bows, as well as crossing over and twirling.

While my eyes filled with tears of pride for our Royal Canadian Mounted Police, I thought back to my fateful coaster ride—which also featured sharp and differing angles, twirling circular action and death-defying drops. I grinned. Then I secretly checked my bra to make sure it was still in place!

Don't Kick
the Bucket

by
Rebecca MacKenzie

Kevin was my favorite cousin. He was six weeks older than me and always in charge. Even though I was younger, and a girl, I was his favorite cousin, too. We were best buddies and we had each other's back. Except for that one memorable day.

I was visiting him at his house. I really liked his house because it had a huge yard and outbuildings, even though it was in the middle of a small town. We were running outside, playing, and enjoying the unbridled energy and carefree shenanigans of typical 10-year-olds. The white-hot sky drove us into the coolness of the huge garage, a barn-like structure that no longer served its original purpose, but was now filled with intriguing miscellanea.

As always, Kevin was the one to initiate mischief. Among the clutter and debris, he had found some twine and proceeded to tie a perfect slip knot. He got a tall bucket and inverted it to serve as a makeshift stool. Climbing atop, he threw the twine over a low rafter and secured it tightly. Then, he slid the knot so that a noose grew larger and larger—eventually so large his head fit right through it. With his head through the noose and standing atop that inverted bucket, he said, "Now, Becky, don't kick the bucket," in a way that I perceived as a challenge.

So, of course, I stepped right over to that bucket and kicked it for all I was worth.

The deed was done. The bucket flew out from under his feet and the noose cinched his windpipe. Probably knowing his dare would be taken literally, Kevin had kept his fingers between the twine and his flesh and luckily, judging by the speed with which his feet were running through the air, the noose had failed to break his neck.

"Put the bucket back! PUT THE BUCKET BACK!!" he croaked, his voice strained and raspy, unable to sustain itself with so little air.

From my comfortable and safe perspective, all this was hilarious. Kevin's desperate running in air, his elbows sticking out at right angles to his body in a futile attempt to pull the noose loose, his head flopping side to side with his large nose airbrushing the ceiling—it was too comical. My always-in-charge cousin was totally at a loss for control. I, too, was at a loss for control, laughing so hard I wet my pants—the *ultimate* humiliation.

"I'll put the bucket back if you promise not to tell that I peed myself!" I bargained. Ironically, I didn't care if he told on me for kicking the bucket and putting him in this dangerous position. I was too young to recognize the life-threatening danger my best buddy was in. I just didn't want anyone to know I'd wet my pants!

"I promise! I promise! Put the bucket back! Put the bucket back!" he rasped, willing to promise anything for the return of solid footing.

I retrieved the bucket and his feet settled on it. He loosened the noose and sat down on the troublesome pail. Rubbing his neck, he studied me with a familiar scowl—the one he always wore when I had not satisfied his expectations. The scowl morphed into a look of realization when he saw my saturated pants.

"You wet your pants!"

"You promised not to tell!" I panicked as the situation reversed itself and focused on my humiliation.

The entire life-threatening episode was behind us as Kevin pushed through the door of the gallows-room and returned to the sunny yard. One of his friends happened to be biking past.

"Hey, Zach! Guess what! Becky wet her pants!"

In retrospect, I guess a little humiliation on my part was a small price to pay for the skin-of-our-teeth escape we made that day. Consequences for our recklessness could have been significantly worse. However, I'm not sure Kevin, my now sky-diving, canyon-hiking, reef-exploring cousin, learned *anything* from the experience.

Been There, Bared That

by
Terri Duncan

We were young and smart. We were invincible. And we would never be caught. At least that's what my brother and I thought. Unfortunately, we didn't give my mother the credit she so deserved. Soon we not only aged very quickly, but we also learned that we were not quite as brilliant as we thought, we most certainly were vulnerable, and boy, did we get caught.

We lived in Georgia. As happens each season, when spring slowly turns to summer, the lure of the local waterhole—Clark Hill Lake—with its cool waters was always too powerful to ignore. Hordes of teenagers flocked to the lake as soon as the frost melted, including my brother and me.

This one day was particularly hot. A group of our friends was camping on the shores of the lake, so my brother and I decided to visit their site. Now, in Georgia, camping at the lake also means partaking in other activities like satisfying thirst with ice-cold beer. When you give a group of naïve teenagers some beer, they drink a lot. And when teenagers consume multiple beers, they tend to lose their ability to think. And when teenagers lose their ability to think, they do dumb things like dare each other to go skinny-dipping in the middle of the day while at a crowded campground. And some slightly inebriated teenagers might just take that dare and get caught by park rangers who strongly recommend the immediate use of swimsuits as well as the consumption of sodas.

In my defense, I was completely submerged under the water when I accepted the dare. The only body part visible was my naked arm wildly waving my little bitty string bikini like a flag. Truly, I figured that it really did not cover much anyway, so what was the harm in revealing just a wee bit more skin?

Needless to say, after the park ranger's visit, the entire group of teenagers—IQs newly restored—adhered to the advice of the campground's law enforcement and spent the rest of the afternoon fully clothed and blissfully sober, thanks to the consumption of Coca Cola rather than PBR! On the way home, my brother and I made a solemn pact never to speak of our momentary lapse of judgment. What happened at the lake would stay at the lake.

Unfortunately, we should also have included our friends in our pact, for the very next day, while I was at my part-time job, the phone rang at my house. One of our camping friends, anxious to relive the experience, immediately began discussing the escapades as soon as the telephone was answered by my mother. In his haste to discuss our youthful frolic in the water, he failed to notice that the female voice on the other end of the line did not belong to me. Nor did my mother, anxious to hear more details of the lake trip, which had been described to her by her two teens as, "You know, it was OK—nothing special," bother to reveal that she was not me. It was only after he reminisced about cold beer and flying bathing suits that he realized how truly quiet "I" was. Only then did he bother to ask, "Uh, is this Terri?" And only then did Momma say, "No, dear. This is Mrs. Ashley." And with that, the conversation abruptly ended.

Thankfully, since I was at work when that fateful call came through, Momma got to my brother first. And my brother happened to be a far better and more skilled liar than me. Without effort, he convinced her that our friend's call was planned and that the group conspired to make the prank call just to see her reaction. Thank goodness she bought the lie hook, line and sinker.

Maybe Momma was so easily swayed because she adored my partner-in-crime. He was her youngest child and only son. Why, her little boy would never do anything so foolish! My brother also managed to track me down at work and prepared me for her inquisition. Crisis averted!

I should say that I learned a great deal from this experience, but that would be a big damn lie. I still drink occasionally—for medicinal purposes only, of course. And I certainly require a great deal of medicine! It would also be a bit of a stretch to suggest that I never again removed a bathing suit while swimming. Technically, the next incident did occur in our backyard in the children's wading pool and only lasted until the mosquitoes started biting. There truly have been no public escapades!

Though I am now much older and perhaps a little

wiser, in retrospect, I would not change a thing that day at the lake. Come to think of it, I would probably still take that dare, even now in my old age, as long as my brother accompanied me. He's still a great liar, and I am certain that Momma still loves him more!

Terri (standing) and Skip

Skip, Andria Ashley (Moma) and Terri

Too Far

by
Betty Guenette

My friends in sixth grade weren't bad, but they sure were foolish. The older eighth graders bragged about tipping over the outside toilets and soaping the windows of darkened houses on Halloween, but not us. Our group of five girls was in the "I-dare-you" stage, and we believed that the challenges we posed to one another made us infinitely braver than those older kids. Suggested dares could arise at any moment and from any one of us, and we rarely anticipated the consequences.

One wintertime dare was that we all hold our breath until we passed out, and when I told my friends that it would be stupid, an alternative suggestion was that we stick our tongues on the frigid metal school fence.

"Why?" someone asked. "That's for kids."

"You're just scared," another girl jeered. "I double dare you."

We all lined up. I stood in back, hoping the end-of-recess bell would ring. No such luck.

After taking a turn, each girl clamped a hand against her mouth. A few tongues stuck so fast that they had to work them off the wire with their fingers. Tears trickled down some frosty cheeks. I filled my mouth with saliva before trying to work my tongue into a point.

"No fair," one of the girls yelled. "You're just going to stick the tip of your tongue on."

"What rule says how much? We just do it." Of course my tongue stuck, too. I tried easing away, but that hurt. I managed to yank my head back with my fingers tight against the sides of my tongue. Faster was better. The split at the tip of my tongue hurt all day, and I spied the others making discreet sucking motions during class the rest of the afternoon. I wasn't the only miserable one.

Our daring adventures were not confined to the schoolyard, though. On Saturdays, our mothers let us go shopping at a nearby department store, often with a few quarters, which bought a lot back then. We usually got an extra nickel for when we needed to use the bathroom. In Canada, you used to have to pay to use the stalls, but we preferred to keep the nickel to buy more treats. One girl dared the others to crawl under the stall doors even if they didn't have to pee. Although we tried to jiggle the slots to shake out nickels, our reward was only a few coins. We didn't think of it as stealing—we were simply being adventurous!

Later, when the store owners caught on to our—and surely others'—antics, they attached another slab of metal at the bottom to prevent peeing without paying, but that didn't stop us from trying. The skinnier girls in our group could still wiggle themselves under the door, but being taller and slightly heavier than my peers, I got wedged. At least I had tried to go feet first. After much tugging, my friends slid me back out—with a ripped blouse and minus some belly skin. When I think about what must have been on those bathroom floors and doors back then, I can't believe how foolish we were—or that I never contracted any serious illness!

During the summer of our sixth-grade year, our dares had escalated in riskiness. With so many lakes surrounding our town, swimming was our most common activity. We soon tired of simply jumping off the rock called "Geronimo," and that's when one of the girls spoke up with a mischievous leer. "I dare you all to dive."

"It's too steep and risky here," I protested, looking around for a safer spot. "Let's go over to that smaller rocky area. The shoreline's level and the water's deep enough." We tried diving at the new location. All of us belly-flopped—no future Olympians in this group—and I fared the worst. You needed to be coordinated for that stuff, and coordination was not my specialty. But I'd get them back. "I double dare you to somersault."

They frowned and looked at each other then back at me.

"OK, you don't have to do a complete somersault," I said, "just flip over and go in feet first."

Each of them took a long time to get ready. They landed wrong and fell in a tangle of flailing arms and legs, some sideways, others butt first. No one was graceful.

"Let's see how good you are," one girl jeered.

I'd show them. While I watched my friends' performances, I realized that we needed running space and a good takeoff to get enough height to flip over. Stepping farther back and taking off at a run, I leapt into the air and twisted my body in an arc—but came down too fast. I landed flat on my back, smacking down hard on the water's surface.

Pain numbed any reaction. I sank to the bottom. I wanted to die. I must have gasped upon hitting the water because I soon choked, spit out water and inhaled another mouthful of water. I needed air, fast. I propelled myself up with wild kicks and hand thrusts.

When I surfaced, the girls grabbed my arms and dragged me onto the rocks where I heaved, gagged and vomited water.

They all looked horrified. "We thought you'd drowned."

"I . . . wanted . . . to," I wheezed. After a few minutes of coughing, vomiting and deep breathing, I got my wind back and could talk. I announced my newfound resolution to the group. "I'm not playing these stupid games anymore."

"You were the one who suggested it," one girl said.

"I know, but we keep trying to outdo our last dare!"

After that truly frightening incident, whenever anyone in our group dared to dare, the rest squelched her. I think we all recognized that if we had continued those escalating challenges, the next dares might have led to smoking, drinking and drugs. Our adventurous grade-school episodes may have been foolish, but they were still innocent enough. I suppose we all mutually realized that it was time to go on to other pursuits—maybe even time to start growing up.

Betty

Leap of Faith

by
Kristen Shalosky

"I don't think this is such a good idea," said my best friend, Elana, referring to my latest dare.

Elana was the voice of reason, as always. And she was probably right, but I was definitely not going to admit it. "You always say that," I sighed out loud.

"And how many times have I been right, Kristen?"

Truth be told, Elana's record was uncanny.

We were smack dab in the middle of what could have been a lazy Florida summer. The unrelenting heat and our empty wallets left my gang of friends short on entertainment options and at age 15, I was far too restless to sit around in the A/C. Instead, I fearlessly led our crew through one idiotic stunt after another, to Elana's constant chagrin.

She had urged me not to be the test subject when we wanted to find out if duct tape could hold a person to a tree.

That experiment played out marvelously, until I had to rip off the tape, taking my flesh with it, only to get down and discover about a hundred splinters in my back.

When I challenged my 13-year-old brother, Michael, to drink a gallon of milk in an hour with me, Elana warned that it wouldn't end well. I, of course, ignored her completely, called Michael a pussy for drinking too slowly, and chugged like a frat boy at homecoming. After spending an hour bent over the toilet—projectile vomiting—I could concede that she had had a point.

And, you know, maybe she had been right to advise against the homemade tattoo gun venture the week before. Thank God the ink we used wasn't as permanent as we'd thought; otherwise, Michael might still have that raggedy flower on the top of his foot.

I dismissed Elana's warning. "It's not that far down," I said to Michael. Surprisingly, this wasn't my dare, but a stunt that had been Michael's idea. I could hardly conceal my pride when he told us about it. He had found a sudden desire to jump off the roof of our two-story house into the backyard grass.

We'd recently discovered an easy path to the roof through an upstairs window and had thus far used the space for sunbathing. I thought this mission was a brilliant way to pump some adrenaline into the otherwise bland day ahead, but now that the time for action was nearing, Michael seemed unsure. So the three of us stood at the edge of the roof, squinting in the midmorning sun at the patch of lawn below us.

Hesitation is for suckers.

"It's pretty far. Have you ever fallen that far?" Elana retorted, skeptically.

I pretended not to hear her.

"You'll be fine, kiddo. Just don't land on the grill. And roll when you hit the ground," I advised, authoritatively.

In the Army's Airborne School, soldiers are taught to roll as they land so that the impact is spread over multiple points of contact. This technique reduces the risk of injury to any individual joint. The worst way to land, in fact, is the way that seems instinctive—on your feet, with your knees straight. I knew all this because my father had told me about it once, but I hadn't the slightest bit of practical experience with it. Still, I relayed the concept matter-of-factly to my companions, feigning expertise.

Elana sighed and turned away, utterly unconvinced. I watched the wheels turn in Michael's head as he weighed his waning faith in me against Elana's logic. It seemed to be quite a struggle. I decided to switch my tactic to all-out peer pressure.

"You ready to make this happen? We'll count for you . . . 3 . . . 2 . . ."

"I . . . I don't know!" he blurted, backpedalling a couple of steps.

I sighed and retreated. How anti-climactic.

Maybe it was part of a deep-seated need to impress my younger brother. Or a twisted manifestation of the massive, closeted crush I was nursing on Elana. But I felt it my absolute responsibility to keep up the chaos and excitement in our lives. And in uncertain times like these, when others wavered, it was my obligation to plunge headlong into the challenge at hand.

"All right, I'll go first," I offered.

Michael looked immediately relieved to be out of the scope of my bullying. Elana shook her head once again—she was beginning to resemble a naysaying bobblehead—and revived her campaign, half-heartedly.

"Kristen, I really don't think this is a good idea."

It's not that I truly disagreed with her. Elana was sensible, mature and probably completely right. But life wasn't about being right; it was about feeling alive. And, more importantly, having bragging rights and badass stories to tell. After all the juicy buildup, Michael's idea to jump off the roof was like a double-dog dare. I couldn't let it pass.

Besides, I had already worked this one out. The key was not locking your knees. I knew how to roll.

"It'll be fine. I'll be fine."

"One day, you'll listen to me," Elana offered wearily, but she didn't even sound like she believed it. Michael had gotten quiet and now just watched the drama unfold expectantly.

"One day. Maybe."

I flashed her a toothy grin then turned dramatically and took a couple of bounding strides toward the ledge.

Countdowns are for suckers.

The argument no longer mattered. I was an unstoppable object in motion and my leap was inevitable. Honestly, I didn't think much at all, except to remind myself to roll. I wondered for a fleeting second right before I jumped how well that technique might work without a parachute, but pushed the thought from my mind. No time for that now.

At the precipice, I planted both feet and sprung into the air heroically with a tremendous *whoosh*—then a sudden, thunderous, bone-trembling thud. And then complete, empty blackness.

As it turns out, 9.8 meters per second squared—my rate of descent—is really fast. So fast, in fact, that I couldn't even formulate a conscious thought in my rush to collide with the earth. I managed to avoid the grill and even bend my knees, but I missed a key piece of information: parachuters roll sideways, not forward, so that they distribute the impact through their feet, ankles, knees, hips and shoulders, in turn. I distributed the impact instead through my feet to my knees and face, a fact that I later confirmed through the face-shaped bruise that ripened on my thigh.

I regained consciousness slowly, wondering at first how I'd ended up in such a peculiar posture. Then I glimpsed Elana and Michael peering down at me from the roof and remembered. I felt an extraordinary amount of pain but couldn't determine its source. For a moment, my body's demand for me to lie still battled my desire to walk it off out of dogmatic pride. Then I imagined trying to justify the situation if my parents discovered me in a crumpled heap next to the Charbroil. I forced myself up and tried to stride around the corner, acting unaffected.

"Should I go?" Michael called out from the roof.

"NO!" I half-shouted, half-whimpered, a bit too emphatically and nasally to maintain my illusion. They disappeared from view and dashed downstairs.

We met in the bathroom, because, of course, cover-up was always priority. My nose was streaming blood and starting to bruise, but miraculously I didn't seem to have broken anything. I tipped my head back to stop the bleeding while Elana dug a cracked bottle of foundation from the dusty graveyard of makeup under my sink. She shook her head slightly as she looked me over. Though she didn't utter a word, I detected a faint I-told-you-so smirk tucked under her expression of concern. It was a face I'd recognize many times in the years to come.

Amazingly, my parents didn't find out about this particular stunt until years later. It was after the stupid kid statute of limitations had passed that Michael and I confessed to a volume of antics. Still, the consequences of the jump and its cover-up were immediate. I woke the next morning with a horrendous headache and whiplash in my neck, just in time for a World Cup party at my soccer coach's house. Every U.S. goal was bittersweet, as I hid my cringing through the high fives and chest bumps, trying desperately not to look too stiff.

But, hey, getting caught is for suckers.

Kristen and Michael

Smart Kids—
Stupid Stuff

Stories about times when we realized
just how lucky we were!

Hitching to Woodstock

by
Francine Baldwin-Billingslea

It was a hot, lazy summer day as I parked my bicycle outside the store and went in to get a cold soda. As I dug in my pockets for change, I couldn't help overhearing a conversation—this tall, long-haired, good-looking guy was telling the store-owner's son he was going to Woodstock. I can remember him saying, "Yeah, man, it's gonna be on a big farm or something. Hendrix and a few other groups are gonna be there. If you wanna come, let me know. It's in a few weeks and it's gonna be a real groovy scene."

I couldn't help myself; I just had to ask. "Hey, you talking about Jimi Hendrix?"

The young man turned around, looked over his square skinny-rimmed sunglasses, and answered, "Yeah, man—the one and only. It's gonna be cool." He then turned his attention back to the owner's son and their conversation.

I opened my soda and sat in a nearby booth, still listening attentively to the two.

"No, we're gonna hitch our way up."

"Maybe I can take my dad's car."

"Yeah, man, that'll be cool. Let me know."

Then they started talking in almost a whisper until the owner's son yelled out, "Five dollars!"

"Yeah, man, this is the best," the handsome man said, as he reached into a small duffle bag and handed him something.

The owner's son looked over at me and said, "The soda's 25 cents. Pay up and get out. I'm closing the store for lunch!"

As I paid the quarter—mostly in pennies—I reminded him that his father never closed the store for lunch. The son reminded me that he wasn't his father, as he practically pushed me out the door while his friend took a seat at the counter.

The year was 1969, I was 14 and thought I was cool and hip, and from the conversation between the two young men, the cool-and-hip place to go was Woodstock—and I wanted to go. That night as I lay in bed, all I could think about was Jimi Hendrix, Woodstock and how I could get there.

The next day, I told my best friend about it. She loved the idea—she wasn't going to ask if she could go, she'd just go. I figured my parents wouldn't want to go, wouldn't take us, nor would they give me permission, so I decided I'd just go also and deal with the consequences later. After all, Woodstock was in New York. We lived less than an hour away from the city. We went there all the time, and I had family who lived in several boroughs. I included my cousin in on our plan, and soon the three of us were excitedly planning our one-day trip to Woodstock.

Part of our planning included asking the store-owner's son about how to get there. When we asked, he told us we were too young to go. We told him we didn't ask him that—we wanted to know if he knew what bus to take. We also wondered if he could ask his friend for any information that would be helpful and to let us know.

He said he wouldn't and that he didn't want to see our ugly faces in the store anymore, and he certainly didn't want to see them at Woodstock. We told him not only was he ugly, but he was mean and we were going to tell his father how he was treating us. He then said if we weren't buying anything, to get out. I sarcastically asked, "Why? Is it time for lunch?"

He turned red and yelled, "Woodstock ain't that far from here. If you really want to go, ride your bikes. Now, get out!"

Dissatisfied we didn't get all the information we wanted, nonetheless we were happy to learn we could ride our bikes. That took care of the transportation part of our plan. Now we needed a contact. My cousin suggested we call our other cousin who lived on Long Island. He was older—about 18 or 19—and cool and hip, too. He'd know about Woodstock, and if he was going, we could probably go with him.

After several days of frantically trying to reach him, he finally called us back. Sounding groggy and irritated, he said, "Yeah, I'm going, but it's not the scene for you." He then said we couldn't go with him and we couldn't ride our bikes. "It's in New York, but upstate and five or six hours away from you. You really need to scratch that idea. I gotta go. Peace." Then he hung up.

Determined now more than ever that we were going to

Woodstock, for the next three weeks my friend, cousin and I baby-sat, saved our allowance, collected and took soda bottles back to the store for the refunds, and emptied out our piggy banks. A few days beforehand, we took our change and earnings to the bank and walked out with over $40 among the three of us.

Since we were going to a farm, we figured we had more than enough money. And because of the distance, we decided to hitchhike. Everybody was doing it and, in all honesty, we were too young and dumb to even think about the danger.

Finally, the momentous day came. While our parents were at work, we dressed in fringed jean shorts, previously tie-dyed and now cut-up T-shirts, and tied scarves around our heads, Jimi-Hendrix style. We went to the store and loaded up on candy, chips and drinks for our trip and were glad to see that the owner was back. We had gotten really tired of arguing with his son every day and before leaving the store, we told him so. Then we walked a few blocks away, stood on the curb, stuck out our thumbs and hoped nobody we knew in our extremely small town saw us.

Car after car passed, some of the folks honked, some waved, some slowed up and then, as if changing their minds, sped off. An older neighbor pulled over and yelled, "I don't know what you girls think you're doing, but you better take your tails home, now!" Later, a friend's brother pulled up and asked us where we were going. In excitement and in unison, we quickly answered, "Woodstock!" He laughed and said, "Yeah, right," before speeding off.

We walked a bit, and then sat on a bench to eat and drink

our snacks and discuss our dilemma. We also discussed the punishment we knew would await us when we got home. But seeing and hopefully meeting Jimi Hendrix would be well worth it.

The day was moving on, which made us anxious. We had been hitching for hours, with no luck. Even though we hadn't gotten anywhere, we agreed we had come too far to give up. We walked a little farther, stood on the curb and once again stuck out our thumbs, praying the rest of the town's folks wouldn't see us.

Finally, an older man pulled up and asked, "Hey, where you going?" When we answered, he said, "Well, you're in luck. That's where I'm heading. Jump in."

I jumped into the front seat, and my cousin and friend in the back seat.

"So, are you into Hendrix?" I asked the man.

"Hendrix—what's that?" he asked with a puzzled look on his face.

"You don't know who Jimi Hendrix is?!" I yelled in surprise.

"Yeah, oh yeah, I know who you're talking about. So, how old are you girls, and are you from around here?

My friend quickly replied, "We're 18, and no, we're not."

He continued with his questions. "Do your parents know you're going to this Woodstock?"

"Yeah," came the backseat answer.

"So, do you girls have boyfriends?"

"Yeah—they're meeting us there," I answered.

He looked over at me, laughed, and then placed his hand on my leg. "You're a real cutie. I think this is gonna be a lucky day for all of us." I looked at him in disgust, rolled my eyes and pushed his hand away.

My cousin asked, "Do you know how to get to Woodstock?"

There was silence, and then he asked, "Do you?"

"Of course! I just wanted to know if you knew," she replied.

"Ah, and I also know a shortcut," the man said. "We'll be there in about an hour. Hey, I have to stop and pick up a friend and get some things for the trip. I want you girls to come in and have a few drinks and smokes with us. It'll make the trip fun, and that's what you girls are looking for, fun, right?"

"We don't drink or smoke, and we'll wait in the car," I sternly responded.

He turned to me with an angry look on his face and said sharply, "You're a bit uptight, aren't you. You definitely need something to mellow you out, and I have just what you need!" He drove a few more blocks before he parked, looked up and down the street, and then at the three of us. Now smiling, he said, "Wait here, I'll only be a minute, and then we'll be on our way to ah . . . ah . . . ah . . . Woodstock, to have some fun and to see this Hendrix guy." He jumped out, ran down the street and disappeared around the back of a house.

Once he was out of sight, I turned to my friend and cousin and yelled, "Come on, let's get the hell outta here!" We jumped out and ran as if we were running for our lives. Luckily, we were only three towns away and were somewhat familiar with the area. We stopped at a Woolworth's to hide, rest, eat a hot dog and drink a soda before catching a bus home.

Safe and sound back home, we sat on my friend's porch

and talked about the strange man and our day. We all agreed that Woodstock probably wasn't a good place for us 14-year-olds, but in hindsight, it would have been great to have been part of an event that is forever engrained in the history of our country. It would have been cool, man—really cool.

Tactical Tomatoes

by
Robert Drummond

How it all got started late one summer I cannot recall. Once started, though, it went from a passing prank to an out-of-control pastime. Somebody, and surely not me, thought it would be better to toss tomatoes at cars rather than eat them, so along with three cohorts, we started our campaign of Tomato Car Puree.

After school we walked the alleys looking for promising beds of tomatoes. Once located, we would return just after dark to make a raid. Neighborhood gardens kept us well supplied with ripe tomatoes, the perfect missiles as far as we were concerned. We flung tomatoes at cars during the nighttime hours from three different locations, each with its own special story.

One prime throwing area was from the alley just behind my house, an alley which intersected with a busy street that curved around the alley's end. Timing was critical. When we saw headlights coming around the curve, we let the tomatoes fly, anticipating the juicy *thwack!* of a hit. We discovered this to be a drawback regarding which cars were selected as we could not see the vehicle until the bombardment was completed.

One evening, seconds after hurling a barrage of tomatoes at an oncoming car, we realized we were throwing at a police car. "Uh oh!" I exclaimed as I heard the *splat!* of tomatoes hit the police cruiser. Unlike other cars, the police car never stopped or even slowed down. We instinctively knew that the cop was just being cool under fire and would return. We ran to my garage next to the alley and hid inside. Looking out a garage window, we saw a police car with its lights out and a policeman walking down the alley toward us. We somehow managed to stay calm, avoiding detection that night. The unspoken message: move on, you've worn out this location—it's too risky now. But that night would come back to haunt us.

Tomato-Throwing-Area-Number-Two was a parking zone located between an old house and the National Guard Armory; the alley behind it gave us an escape route. We blasted quite a few cars before leaving this area after a particularly memorable night. One dark evening as we prepped our mushy ammo, we were distracted by the light in the bedroom of the old house. Without a word, we watched as an attractive woman entered the room. She was undressed, and we could see her husband in the bathroom shaving. The woman faced us as she sat on the bed and began dressing, and even though we knew she could not see us, we nevertheless stopped in our tracks.

Watching her putting on those nylons really got our attention, and once we resumed breathing, we decided to climb onto the owner's wooden fence to get a better view. Alas, our combined weight caused a part of the fence to collapse, making a very loud racket. This scared us off, though the thrill of our unintentional peep show was worth it. But it was time to move on to another location.

The last area we selected for our tomato flinging had many advantages—from a macabre point of view, that is. We positioned ourselves along a stone wall inside a cemetery. The street that paralleled the wall offered many great targets of opportunity. Although one motorist was brave enough to hop over the wall and give us a short chase, and many others who stopped unleashed some rather nasty verbal comments, we always managed to make it home unscathed. At that time, my right leg was in a walking cast due to a knee injury, and it extended from my upper thigh down to my ankle. All of my friends promised repeatedly that they would stay with me in case of trouble, a commitment that was severely tested the night we tomato terrorists threw one tomato too many.

The second motorist who jumped over the cemetery wall to chase us was different from the first. We took off running—I, in my cast, peg-legged it as fast as I could.

Suddenly I heard a male voice yelling, "Stop or you're dead!" followed quickly by three gun shots. Flashlights were everywhere, as were the police. My buddies were nowhere in sight. Using my high-school military training, I remembered how to hide from the enemy. I dropped under a large spruce tree, hiding my face and hands as best as I could.

Soon, a policeman with one of my friends in tow came right by me. "Where are the rest of your friends?" the policeman demanded.

"That's all," my loyal pal kept insisting.

After a while, I sensed that everyone had left; I found myself scared and quite alone in the cemetery. It was a long walk home that brisk night.

By the next morning the word was out. My three friends had been hauled down to jail and their parents had to come get them. "Where were you?" my mother asked over and over. She knew I was involved, even though I tried to deny it. As punishment, my captured friends had to spend Halloween eve and Halloween night in the city jail, and I—still claiming innocence—had to stay home because of my suspected role. My parents were not about to let me talk my way out of this one.

We later learned that four patrol cars and seven policemen were involved in attempting to catch us—the wily tomato throwers. It turns out that the police had been quite upset for some time, especially since one policeman was hit in the neck through an open window at the first tomato-pegging location.

The saga ended, my vegetable-launching days were over, but my mom kept the story of that incident alive. When she finally got me to confess my role in that night's shenanigans, wondering how I was able to escape when everyone else got caught, I told her that I had fallen into an open grave and had hidden there before later crawling out. She bought my slightly embellished story, passing it along as truth for the amusement of family and friends for years!

Robert

Monkey Business

by
Dana Reynolds

"Please do not feed the monkeys," I read aloud on that hot summer day.

When I was 12, my family visited one of those zoos that had the animals in what appeared to be train cars. Being at an awkward age, I felt a special kinship with the monkeys that year. My family moved on to the next car, but I remained behind to bond with the various monkeys and other primates.

Signs all around advised, "Do not feed the monkeys." Another sign read, "Please remain behind the second fence." There was a waist-high fence that was intended to keep visitors several feet back from the actual cages. "Stay Back!" the sign on this fence warned. To a 12-year-old, those signs sounded like good advice—for other people. These monkeys were my friends now. And, come to think of it, they looked a bit hungry.

Having no snacks with me, I reasoned that perhaps monkeys would enjoy grass. After all, they were from the jungle—surely they would enjoy a handmade monkey salad! And enjoy it they did, although it seemed rather inconvenient for all of us that I had to throw handfuls of grass 3 feet through the air, and the monkeys had to pick up individual blades of grass from the cage floor. Wouldn't it be much better to hand the bundles of grass to my new best friends?

In true monkey fashion, I hoisted myself up so that my knees were resting on the fence. I leaned forward toward my favorite chimp's cage, braced myself by grabbing one of the bars with my left hand, and, with my other hand, reached between the bars to hand a delicious clump of greenery to my adorable new pal.

Our mutual attraction quickly became apparent. We gazed into each other's eyes. I smiled. He smiled back. We began a conversation:

"Want some yummy grass? Do you?" I crooned.

"Grunt," he replied.

"What are you saying, fellow, huh?"

"Grunt! Grunt! Grunt!" he responded, cocking his head as if considering my worthiness.

If being judged monkey-worthy is a plus, I won the Jungle Lottery that afternoon. The chimp moved his face closer to mine and showed his pearly whites—then lunged! Before I could even think of pulling away, the chimp reached between the bars of the cage, grabbed my right arm just below the shoulder, and yanked for all he was worth. I flailed for a few seconds, lost my balance, fell off the fence that held the "Stay Back!" sign, and then felt myself pulled right up against the bars of the monkey's cage.

I sort of dangled there for a moment, dazed and just beginning to question my own wisdom.

"Um, help?" I tried tentatively.

But the other members of my family had left the monkey car and were several cars away. There were no other visitors at the monkey car with me. I tried to decide whether this was a good thing or a bad thing. The monkey yanked harder. Then harder still. I decided it was a bad thing.

"Help!" I shouted, loudly this time.

(YANK)

"HELLLPPP!" I yelled for all I was worth.

Luckily, my family had missed me, and my older sister was en route back to the monkey car to see what the heck was taking me so long. I will never forget the look on her face when she found out the answer to that question.

"Save me!" I demanded.

She stared at me, open-mouthed. "Ah, how?"

"I don't know! Fight him or something? You watch *Tarzan* movies!"

My brave older sis leapt the fence, grabbed me around the waist and proceeded to engage in a tug of war with the enamored chimp, with yours truly playing the role of the rope. My athletic sibling pulled with all of her might, I pushed on the bars with my monkey-free hand, and eventually we began to gain some ground. Suddenly, we fell backward, knocking over the fence holding the "Stay Back!" sign. I was free! My primate paramour was looking distinctly unhappy, and my right arm had deep scratches from shoulder to wrist.

After a tetanus shot and a deserved scolding, I was as good

as new. My punishment was having to spend the rest of the summer explaining how I got the light-pink marks running the length of the inside of my right arm. Turns out those signs telling us not to feed the monkeys offered pretty good advice. Yes, even for monkey-crazy 12-year-olds!

Backyard Armageddon

by
John Reas

Summers were always the best times for war games. By the time school was out in June, the lines were drawn and our neighborhood became alive with about 10 of us waging battle campaigns across neighborhood yards, tree houses and the playground near our elementary school.

The entire neighborhood became prime territory for conquest, and invariably, my younger brother Paul and I would take opposing sides while we recruited others to join our respective armies. Paul may have had a cool plastic M-16 that looked like something straight from Vietnam and made an awesome *rat-a-tat* sound whenever the trigger was depressed, but I would sneak out with my older brother's ROTC drill rifle. We considered it a draw in the firepower at our disposal.

My friend Pete could be counted on to carry his Red Ryder BB gun into battle, and Dave packed some serious heat with the *Star Trek* assault rifle he carried. And Mike always carried his Napoleon Solo gun from *The Man from U.N.C.L.E.* The rest of the neighbor kids, all between the ages of eight and 10, had arsenals that would have made the NRA proud.

Typically, we would all meet in someone's backyard for a council of war to determine the opposing side and the territories that they owned and would need to conquer. From there, we would fan out on our search-and-destroy missions. Soon, the sounds of gunfire and shouting would erupt. "I got you first!" and "No, you didn't, you couldn't hit an elephant if its butt was in your face!" were the cries that quickly resounded down the alleyways and across the yards of our neighborhood. Unless one was able to sneak up on an opponent and shoot him in the back—which rarely happened—the question of who shot first was always a subject of debate.

While summer outdoor activities kept us occupied for hours on end, nothing could beat the interest Paul and I had in building models. When it came to our birthdays and Christmas gifts, our parents knew that model kits were a slam-dunk road to success. Revell, Tamiya and Monogram—we were completely indiscriminate regarding the brands of kits. Over the years, our bedroom became a museum of historical vehicles, ships and planes to rival the Smithsonian. American Sherman tanks, German Tigers, Japanese Zeros, Messerschmitts, Spitfires, battleships, cruisers, armored personnel carriers, F-4 Phantoms—our arsenal transcended wars.

We also had Army men by the hundreds. Whenever we declared war, there was usually a mad scramble for as many of the green Army men as we could get our hands on, since none of us wanted the nasty gray Germans. Over the years, our infantries were augmented by space creatures, knights on horseback, Roman centurions, Vikings, Union cavalry and Paul's G.I. Joe action figure. Later, as the armies continued to grow, the Six Million Dollar Man joined the fray. Steve Austin may have had his bionic powers, but in our war games, he was just a regular soldier like everyone else.

It was during one of our frequent military endeavors—when every spare inch of our bedroom was crawling with men on the attack and ships, vehicles and planes were fully deployed—that Paul suggested we needed to take our campaign outside.

"We need more space. I don't have enough room to spread out my men," he complained as he was taking chunks of Silly Putty and rolling them into cannonballs. "You know, we could do this in the backyard."

"Good idea. There's the space between the garden and the fence that's perfect for us to set everything up!" I said. I grabbed the men and dumped everything into our dad's old Army footlocker next to the dresser, which was well suited for transporting our arsenel to the backyard for combat.

"We need to bring the models, too," Paul added. He emptied out the laundry basket and started placing tanks and airplanes into it. Soon, we had accumulated a sizable number of items needed for our own World War III. While we were at it, we hauled out our Alamo battle play set, complete with Mexican soldiers in different fighting poses, the toy castle I'd had since the first grade, and other long-forgotten toys hidden in the crevices of the closet. Even our Lincoln Logs and Legos joined the fight.

Over the course of that Saturday August afternoon, the Reas backyard was transformed into a setting for a battle of mythic proportions. It became Gettysburg, D-Day, Midway and Agincourt rolled into one.

By 3 P.M., we were hot, tired and utterly amazed at the incredible array now in place in the backyard. There, interspersed on the dry grass, was every single soldier, sailor, toy creature and model vehicle we had ever built. I even placed my model of the Saturn V rocket behind my lines, waiting to serve as a transport for the squad of Vikings who would be leading a raid on Paul's *Planet of the Apes* figures.

As we were about ready to start the battle, Pete, Mike and Dave wandered up to the fence.

"Whatcha' doin'?" smacked Dave as he carefully blew a bubble from the wad of Bazooka gum he was chewing.

"Just wait," said Paul. "We are about to start a war."

"It's not realistic enough. You need to place mines, have artillery, you know, blow things up," said Mike. "I know where Larry's leftover fireworks are hidden."

We all looked at him. His older brother, Larry, was famous for the sparklers, Black Cats, cherry bombs and M-80s that he managed to scrounge together. By the Fourth of July, Larry could be counted upon to roam the neighborhood with his buddies, terrorizing household pets and other animals as he unleashed Armageddon.

"How much does he have left?" Paul asked.

"Plenty. I mean, this would be like a napalm strike," said Mike. His oldest brother had returned from Vietnam slightly half-crazed and was always telling us kids about the things he saw over there. Napalm seemed to always be interwoven in his accounts when he would sit out on the back stoop of his house, smoking his cigarettes, and retelling us of what life was like on a firebase.

So, with that thought in mind, the group of us trudged over to Mike's house and snuck up into Larry's room. Mike walked in without a care, knowing his brother was out that afternoon, and opened his closet door. He reached in the back and pulled out a large cardboard box.

While Mike was opening the box, Dave looked behind him and said, "Wow, look at this!" He reached down and pulled a *Playboy* from the closet. All eyes grew wide as we huddled around Dave as he paged through it.

Mike looked at us scornfully. "You guys are something else. I thought we came up here for the fireworks. I've seen these before. No big deal." Maybe no big deal for him, but for the rest of us, this was something we never even knew existed!

Suddenly, Mike said, "Crud! I think Larry's back!" Sure enough, we could hear him yelling downstairs to his older brother that he was ready to head off with him. We all held our breath. We then heard the two brothers talking, the sound of a toilet flushing, the backdoor slamming, car doors closing and a car pulling out of the driveway.

With the coast now clear, we hauled the box back to our backyard and unloaded the contents next to the battlefield. It was an impressive collection of pyrotechnics, and we put all of them to great use. By the time we were finished, we had strung firecrackers and sparklers across the yard, burying some beneath the fortifications and underneath all of the plastic models Paul and I had built over the years. It was getting close to 5:30, and we knew we needed to get our war underway before our parents would be expecting all of us home.

I ran into the kitchen, where my mom was preparing a casserole for dinner. "We'll be ready in 20 minutes. You boys need to finish up whatever you're doing out there then come in and wash up."

I mumbled, "Yes'm," as I opened a kitchen drawer and pulled out a box of matches. I ran back to the yard and passed them around. All of us started to light matches, and then the fuses strewn throughout the field of battle.

As the fuses started to sputter, Pete yelled, "Take cover!" We all ran back toward the tool shed next to the garden plot and huddled on the ground. Seconds later, the ground erupted. Pieces of plastic rained down upon us as the remains of tanks, ships, airplanes and military figures were launched into the air. A large string of firecrackers Dave had buried in the dirt between the opposing sides went off with a series of mini explosions that sounded like machine-gun fire. The castle turret teetered and fell while the Alamo blew apart from the force of the M-80 placed underneath it. Nothing survived the carnage, including my Apollo Saturn V rocket that was vaporized by the cherry bomb inserted in its tailpipe. Army men who had been strapped to bottle rockets went into orbit, never to be seen again, while G.I. Joe was dismembered. The noise was so loud it caused every dog in the neighborhood to bark, and caused enough racket to wake the dead.

As the explosions died down, we saw the first flames of fire begin to flicker from the results of our work. Mom ran out of the house, frantic. "What in the world are you boys doing? You just set the yard on fire!" All five of us jumped up and stared where Mom was pointing. The flames were getting larger and spreading fast across the dry August lawn.

"Quick, get the hose and buckets!" Dave yelled.

"My garden!" cried Mom.

In seconds, the five of us were running like loose cannons as Paul grabbed the hose from the side of the house and Pete turned on the faucet. Meanwhile, I ran over to the toolshed and grabbed a couple of buckets and ran to the house to fill them up in the kitchen. Dave and Mike followed me, and as quickly as one was filled, they ran it out to dump it on the grass to contain the rapidly spreading flames. The makeshift bucket brigade continued for several more minutes while Paul and Pete performed their firefighter act. Soon, the flames died down, leaving a scorched backyard and blackened vegetables in the garden.

"My green beans are ruined! And look at my tomatoes!" Mom was absolutely furious as we surveyed the damage of our backyard war. "Boys, go to your room! No supper for both of you. Just wait until your father gets home!"

Dave, Mike and Pete took that opportunity to jump back over the fence and disappear. Paul and I slunk upstairs to our bedroom, which was eerily silent without the models. Our vast collective military might was now scattered across the backyard, the results of the battle to end all battles.

As Paul and I stretched out on the floor to await Dad's arrival and a fate that would surely be worse than death, Paul commented, "Well, it wasn't a total bust this afternoon." With that, he pulled out a crumpled centerfold he had torn out of the *Playboy* magazine before running out of Larry's bedroom. The centerfold playmate was wearing a peace sign necklace, but very little else.

I'd always wondered since that day if we had grabbed the magazines instead of the fireworks, how very differently that afternoon would have ended.

John

When You Gotta Go

by
Pat Nelson

My dad drank a beer now and then. When I was about 10, I remember tasting one of his beers and to me, it was nasty and bitter. This taste had been my only exposure to alcohol, but that all changed four years later.

My best friend Marilyn, a year older than me, brought home a pint of vodka from a vacation in Wyoming. Her much older cousin had supplied the forbidden drink. Marilyn kept the bottle hidden, and we made plans to get together and give it a try it. At ages 14 and 15, we were near-grownups and excited to make such important plans.

Finally, we had the opportunity. "Mom, Marilyn wants to spend the night, OK?"

"I don't see why not," my mother replied.

Marilyn went home and packed her pajamas and toothbrush, plus the bottle of forbidden booze, into her overnight bag. That evening, we could barely control our giddiness as we waited for bedtime. We rode our bikes around the neighborhood until almost dark. The fragrance of newly-harvested mint filled the warm night air. The evening felt magical.

As we rode, we made plans. I had a long, narrow upstairs bedroom running from the front to the back of the house. The stairway was in the middle, and there was a door at the bottom. I usually left the door open, but Marilyn and I knew we would have to close it. And we would have to have some way of knowing if my mother opened the door. We had an idea. After dinner, we said goodnight to my parents and pulled the stairway door closed behind us. Carefully and quietly, we hung a bunch of wire coat hangers on the door so we would know if someone opened it.

Marilyn and I stared at the vodka bottle for a while before opening it. No one had told us about mixers. Marilyn went first. She took a small sip of the straight vodka. It was a little swallow, her eyes got big and she let out a gasp, and then a giggle. Next, I took a taste. The excitement made up for our burning throats and the paint thinner taste. Soon, we rolled with laughter on the bed. And then we had to pee.

Oh, no. What if Mom wanted to talk to us when we went downstairs? We would have to be very quiet and very quick. Silently—as silently as possible, while stifling giggles—we tiptoed down the stairs. In our haste, we threw open the door and were serenaded by clanging coat hangers as they fell to the floor. Wide-eyed, we picked them up and hurried taking turns going to the bathroom.

"What's wrong?" asked Mom from her bed.

"Nothing," I replied. "Marilyn just dropped something. Sorry. G'night."

We closed the stairway door behind us, hung the clothes hangers back on the knob, and covered our mouths with our hands to try to hold in our laughter. We hurried back upstairs and had another swig.

No one ever told us about having to pee a lot when drinking alcohol. It seemed like only minutes passed before we had to go again. We knew we couldn't go back downstairs without arousing suspicion. I looked around my room for a container. There were none. We had only one option—we would have to crawl out the window and onto the roof.

I forced the rusty latch on the window, and as quietly as possible, both of us pushed with all our might to slide up the old wooden frame. It hesitated but did not squeak. Because it was coated with layers of paint, we were able to open it only about 3 feet before it stuck. One by one, we stepped out onto the small, flat, tar-papered roof outside my bedroom window, directly above the front porch. There, we prepared to relieve ourselves, but suddenly realized that the streetlight on the corner shined on us like a spotlight.

Ours was only one house from the corner, and one car after another passed by on the nearby street. Finally, traffic slowed. We quickly pulled down our pajama bottoms, spread our legs and grasped our flannel pajama bottoms to hold them out of the way, and did what we had to do. Then we each pulled up our pants, ducked down, threw a leg over the windowsill and crawled back into my bedroom before anyone saw us.

Suddenly tired from our adventure, we carefully hid the bottle and slipped silently into bed. We'd had an exciting night in the spotlight as *piddlers* on the roof.

Shortcuts

by
Annmarie B. Tait

How, as a child, I always managed to wind up on the "uh-oh" end of one of my mother's many warnings is really no mystery, but it always took me by surprise. And so on a bitter cold day in February, my sister Marie and I set out for school and let my mother's warning of "Don't take the shortcut!" slide right past us without so much as a nod that we even heard her. But I did hear her. I always heard her. I just had a phenomenal knack for making poor choices when it came to following sensible advice, and this day proved no different.

The distance between our elementary school and our front door measured six long city blocks, 15 minutes from start to finish when sauntering at a day-dreaming schoolgirl's pace. Whatever held us up at home that morning, I don't remember. I do remember is watching my sister spin into a panic because we only had 10 minutes to get to school before the bell rang.

Taking the shortcut was our only hope lest we play chicken with the Devil himself and chance being late for school, the consequences of which neither of us had the courage to face. Such was life in Catholic school in the 1960s—arrive on time or else, and the "or else" seemed infinitely more ominous than my mother's barely-acknowledged shortcut concern.

At Marie's first utterance that we consider the shortcut, I jumped right on the offer and shot back, "Let's do it! Let's do it!" And we hurried on our way. The shortcut eliminated a lot of walking by accessing the schoolyard through the back driveway—allowing arrival all the sooner in plain view of the patrolling Sisters of St. Joseph. With no time to squander, we made our decision to ignore Mom's advice.

The snag in this plan was Doc's candy store, a hangout for tough older boys who made sport of hurling wisecracks at innocent passersby. Two scrawny little girls didn't stand a chance scooting past Doc's unscathed, but what's a smart remark or two when your non-tardy reputation hangs in the balance? We forged on.

Hardly were we past Doc's door when a group of boys began fighting. Amid flying fists one boy picked up a jaggedly cut tin-can top from the gutter and hurled it. Once it swished past me I turned toward Marie, and the look on her face most definitely spelled, "Uh oh!" It was then that the little neon sign started blinking in my head: *Don't take the shortcut. Don't take the shortcut.*

Quick as lightning, Marie grabbed my hand and we tore a path to the schoolyard. The bitter cold kept a secret from me, but the frightened faces of the other children said it all as we made our way over to my teacher, Sister Lorraine. Once Sister saw us, she scooped me into her arms and the crimson telltale sign of my injury now smeared across the stiff white bib of her habit. I never cried until I saw the blood, and then noticed my coat and mittens were bloody as well.

Sister carried me to the school nurse who looked up from her desk and gasped. She hastily applied pressure to my cheek to stop the bleeding while Sister called my mother to explain that I had to go to the hospital. Now that I was inside, my cheek began to burn and throb. When the rusty lid whizzed past me, it sliced my left cheek, leaving a fairly deep, lacerated wound in its path. Knowing that Mom was on her way set the oatmeal in my stomach to flip-flopping, and whispers of stitches and a tetanus shot didn't do much to help.

Why didn't I heed Mom's advice? Not only would I be in trouble for disobeying, I was also on my way to the emergency room for stitches and shots. All this just to avoid being late for school. By the time Mom arrived, the nurse had cleaned and bandaged the wound. I caught a glimpse of my reflection in the mirror on the office wall and blood was starting to seep through the bandage. What a gruesome sight!

When Mom saw me, she never even flinched. She took my hand, looked me straight in the eye and said, "Don't you worry, Annie, everything will be all right." That didn't stop me from crying, though. The fear of someone using a needle and thread to stitch my cheek back together had a pretty tight grip on my churning stomach. But I knew that if Mom said everything would be all right—in the end it would be.

Somewhere in the middle of all the confusion I figured out she wasn't angry with me either. Even at seven years old, it was easy for me to see in her eyes that she felt my pain and fear. Her mission was to save me from this anguish and deliver me back to the land of coloring books and cupcake surprises. Just seeing her in the doorway of the nurse's office brought me relief before I ever saw a doctor.

On the way to the hospital, Mom told me that I would probably get a needle that would feel like a prick in my skin. She said that she would hold my hand and that I should squeeze her hand as hard as I could so all the pain would travel through my hand and transfer to her. How amazed I was that such a thing was possible, but more so that she was willing to do that for me.

Although I did end up getting a tetanus shot—while squeezing most of the pain into Mom's hand as she held mine tightly—the doctor applied three butterfly bandages instead of stitches to my check, and the worst was over. I left the hospital holding on to Mom's hand and fully expecting a lecture on the way back about how easily the Devil makes trouble for you when you disobey your mother. To my surprise, that didn't happen at all. When I finally summoned the courage to tell Mom why we took the shortcut, she put her arm around me and said, "I know you didn't mean to disobey me. Sometimes bad choices crop up in a field of good intentions."

I have tucked that lesson about compassion in my heart among all my other treasured memories of Mom, who is long gone, and I am grateful to her whenever I come across an opportunity to put her wisdom to good use.

Sister and Annmarie

Farm Olympics

by
James Butler

For all the athleticism involved in performing the various tasks needed to work a dairy farm, the environment is not very conducive to practicing traditional sports. But there are sporting events unique to farm life that evolved to satisfy competitive urges. I am not talking about rodeo events, as they fall into the Ranch Olympics category. Anyone who ever watched the old westerns knows a farm and a ranch are as different as a swamp and a desert, as are the people who inhabit them.

Probably the best known and most organized farm sport is tossing horseshoes. I was not very good at it. After I pitched one through the window of a new Ford F100 pickup, they would not let me play anymore. What kind of idiot parks a new pickup truck behind a horseshoe pit anyway, even if it was 50 feet away?

There were plenty of running events as well. The dinner sprint from the back-40 tested endurance, while the survival sprint came in handy after throwing a toad at your sister. Then there was the obstacle course used to escape angry parents who caught you doing something stupid. I was always running away from, or after, something. Mom called me "the dusty blur." Farms are always knee-deep in mud or dust—they're a kid's heaven!

My special skills were best suited to a sport few urban dwellers have ever heard of: cow skiing. This does not involve putting a cow on skis or a cow sliding in any fashion. In this sport, Bossy is the power boat, her tail the tow rope, my rubber boots the skis and the knee-deep dust (or mud) the water. The technique was pretty straight forward:

1. Drop a handful of hay in the barnyard so Bossy would stand still for a minute.

2. Slowly walk up behind Bossy and reach out for her tail without touching it.

3. Grab that tail with both hands and scream, "YEE HAH!"

4. Hang on for dear life as Bossy bolts across the barnyard, bellowing in protest.

Oh, man—the thrill, the speed, the dirt in the face, the danger, the rock pile straight ahead. Time to bail out! I let go just in time and tumbled up against the first big stone as Bossy trotted back to the unfinished hay.

Whee, nearly got stoned on that one! Gotta try that again.

Despite its strong similarities to NASCAR racing, cow skiing never gained much popularity as the adults were generally unsupportive. My father hated it. He told me it was because he was afraid I would get hurt really bad. Yeah, right. Like making a nine year old drive a 200 HP farm tractor was not dangerous.

One day he spotted me doing my thing and screamed at me

as I left him in the dust on the obstacle course.

"I see you doing that again, I'm gonna whup you good!"

Only one thing to do: make sure he did not see me. Just one problem—farm dads are not like city dads. They do not go off to work in the morning, leaving their male children to wreak havoc in the neighborhood until they get home. Farm dads can pop up anywhere, anytime, on any day.

One afternoon I heard him talking about needing to go do something on the back-40 and followed him around the barn. I watched through a fence as he climbed on the tractor and took off around the silo.

"Now's my chance!"

I slipped into the barnyard, set up Bossy and took off. Thirty feet later, Dad jumped out from behind the silo, grabbed me by the collar with one hand—nearly strangling me—tossed me over his shoulder and headed for the barn.

"YEEOWW!"

Oh, man, was he right. Cow skiing got me hurtin' really bad! I retired from cow skiing forever. Still, there were some long-term benefits from the Farm Olympics. I had built up a great cardio system running from Dad every time he caught me doing something stupid. After we sold the farm and moved into town, I joined the high school track team where I broke the school, league and district records for the mile run, eventually finishing fifth in the State Championship Meet. Bossy would have been proud.

James

Five generations: Baby James is held by father Lawrence Butler, with Lawrence's father Charles Butler standing. Charles' mother Grace (Butler) Castleman is seated on the arm next to her father, Fred Castleman.

They'll
Never Know

Getting away with it—or not!

B.A.B.

by
John J. Lesjack

"You can't have a swim pass," Mother said, "and that's final!"

I looked up from the landing where I was folding my thick Wednesday newspapers. I did not understand why my mother would not allow me to swim in the clear water of Eastwood Park Pool. Outside temperatures would reach the 90s today. Eastwood Park was only a mile away. I could pay for the pass myself. She could be free of me all afternoon. *What was her real reason for keeping me from the pool?*

"Do you understand what I am telling you, son?" my mother asked.

I frowned and looked at my full canvas bag filled with *Detroit Times* newspapers. "You're saying you don't want me to go swimming because I'm only in the sixth grade."

"I'm saying the park is too far away, and I can't be there to supervise," she countered.

Supervise? I thought. *Supervise?* My mother was embarrassed about not being able to swim and refused to talk about it. Who was she going to supervise anyway—the lifeguards at the pool?

"I'll be home before you finish delivering your newspapers," she said as she left in her black 1941 Hudson to do her shopping in East Detroit. I hauled my Dayton Flyer out of the garage, tied my newspaper bag on the handlebars and pedaled off.

In 1947, a paper route for an 11-year-old was a rite of passage. When you were 10, you had no money. At 11, you had a bicycle, a paper route and an income, even when you grew up without sidewalks or street lights. True, you had to ride one mile from your house out to the country and back, winter and summer, but the trip had its perks. For every nickel paper you sold, you'd earn a three-cent profit.

Half a mile from home, my bike rattled over some railroad tracks into real farmland. Corn grew and cows grazed on one side of the dirt road. On the other side of the road sat three houses in a row and acres of undeveloped rolling countryside with vernal pools filled with rainwater. Often I heard laughter and shouting coming from that area, so once, after I delivered newspapers to my three customers, I walked my bicycle onto a little mound of dirt for a better look at the noisemakers. That was when I saw them.

Two boys, about my age, with totally wet hair, were splashing one another in a pond. They must have attended school down the road because I didn't know them. I went to St. Veronica School where sad-looking nuns tried to convince me everything I did was a sin. I suffered with that concept as I tried to believe the nuns. I really did.

One boy climbed out of the water, smiled, stood on a rock, yelled "Geronimo!" and jumped into the water. Cooling off naturally had great appeal to me until I realized I had not worn my swim trunks . . . and neither had the boys!

"Welcome to Bare Ass Beach!" the second boy yelled to me just before he jumped from the rock.

Embarrassed, I hastened to finish my paper route. When I got home, I tried to concentrate on listening to *The Lone Ranger* on WXYZ radio, but all I could think about was what sins those boys at the swimming hole were committing by swimming in the buff. I ran through the Ten Commandments but found nothing in there about swimming apparel.

Thursday, five boys were swimming at B.A.B., as I called it. All were happily splashing the others, jumping off the rock, or sitting half submerged in the cool water. *If they were sinning, why did they look so happy?* I wondered.

Friday, I finished my route early and saw two boys leaving B.A.B. with wet hair. Their sweaty clothes had dried on their bicycles. They rode away and the pond was empty, inviting and wet. The temperature was about 90 degrees. I had no swim trunks with me, so I decided to do some "sin research." That is, I wanted to find out what it was like to swim *au naturel.*

While my sweaty clothes dried on my bicycle, I slipped into the cool water quietly. Although I was alone in the country, I was naked and thus did not want to risk calling attention to myself. As soon as my bare feet touched the water, I knew I had made a wonderful decision. Pond water can be a little dirty, but it's so very welcome after a hot day of delivering newspapers and hearing complaints about what customers had to do to find the newspapers I had put where they told me to put them. I remember two things about sinking into that little pond of cool water: I felt totally refreshed, and I was surprised that this pond water was clear. No, wait . . . a third thing! How could this be a sin?

That night, as my younger brother Richard and I lay awake in our own beds waiting for sleep, I told him quietly about the "old swimming hole" and that even though you really couldn't swim there, you could get wet and cool off. Naturally, he wanted to go. I told him that if he helped me deliver half my route—30 newspapers—I'd show him where it was. He wanted to know the name of the place. We never knew when Mom was listening to see if we were talking or sleeping, so I whispered, "B.B.B."—"Bare Back Beach."

Saturday, we had the water to ourselves—everyone must have been at the air-conditioned theater watching an afternoon of cowboy movies. Richard quickly hung his clothes on his bicycle, ran over to the rock, yelled, "Look out below!" and did a cannonball. His tremendous splash put me to shame so I pushed a larger rock into place, leapt high from that rock and made the best splash of my life. Richard and I were both standing on our rocks when we heard a familiar car horn honking. *Uh oh! Busted!*

Our mother was parked on the road, yelling, "Get your clothes on this instant! And get home! You're both going to confession!" She must have been listening to us talk last night. She had driven me around during snowstorms, so she knew my route. My fear of my mother—an immigrant farmer's daughter—was greater than my fear of hell, so when the confessional panel slid open, I quickly followed the program I had been taught. "Bless me, Father..."

"Well, Johnny, why are you here?" the priest asked.

Sheepishly, I confessed, "My mother sent me and told me to tell the truth."

"What have you done?"

I wanted to argue that Adam and Eve didn't wear clothes, but I kept my confession simple. "I went swimming," I said, suddenly embarrassed.

"Swimming?" the priest repeated. "Swimming is not a sin. Was it a *special* kind of swimming?"

I thought quickly and said, "My mother said swimming at B.B.B. was a sin and I had to tell it in confession, Father."

"B.B.B?" the priest repeated. "I'm not familiar with that place. What do the letters stand for?"

"Bare Back Beach," I said, softly. I had considered telling him the real name, but I thought better of it.

The priest went quiet. I know now that I had not fooled him at all. He had paused to laugh without making a sound and to get control of himself before he could talk. But back then, as I waited and waited, I conjured up all sorts of punishments that would be coming my way for having not done anything wrong. Finally, before he slid the panel shut, he said, "Say three Hail Marys and make a good Act of Contrition."

When we got home from church, my brother and I found swim passes and new swim trunks on our beds. Monday, while Richard played in the pool's shallow water, I did something my mother could never do: I jumped off the high board. When I climbed out of the pool dripping wet, my mother waited for me.

"When I saw you jump off the high board," she said, "my heart was in my throat. And when you didn't surface right away, I wanted to call the lifeguard."

"I like to touch the bottom of the pool and shove off," I said. "It takes a while to get to the deep part."

What I didn't tell her was what I especially liked about jumping off the high board into clear water was that, afterwards, I didn't have to go to confession for doing something I truly enjoyed doing.

Little Johnny

Truth or Consequences

by
Kathleene S. Baker

I was 14 years old and in awe as I blossomed on the pathway to becoming a woman. Going through the ugly, awkward phases had left me terrified of what the outcome might be. Eventually, my confidence began to build as curves took shape where they should and I no longer looked like a little girl.

That particular summer, the youngest of my older brothers purchased a ski boat. Most weekends, he and friends went to nearby lakes for a day of skiing and likely spent as much time chasing girls as they did boating. However, now and then, when my brother and a long-time family friend were going alone, I was invited and Mother was comfortable with me joining them.

Skiing filled me with excitement. I loved jumping wakes, swinging alongside the boat, and when I mastered the slalom, I was in hog heaven. Not to mention, I felt I must be developing OK for the guys to drag me along—out in public, no less. I mean, I was just a kid hanging out with 20-year-olds!

After several excursions that went well, I was again asked to spend Saturday on the lake with the boys. Mother agreed, and I counted the days until I'd be back up on water skis jumping wakes. On Thursday morning, though, I thought the world had come to an end—I had started my period a week early!

"Mom, what am I going to do?" I asked her, nearly in tears. "I want to go skiing!"

She didn't offer much comfort. "I'm sorry, Kathy, I don't see how you can. A pad is bound to be visible in your bathing suit."

I was a bit wiser than she realized, so when she didn't mention tampons, I did! Merciful heavens—I swear she swooned.

"You know, I've never even used tampons and I'm not sure they are suitable for unmarried women."

Her reply didn't satisfy me in the least. I was hell-bent on going to the lake.

"Mom, I've read advertisements in magazines and have never read *that*."

After some discussion and my fussing, Mother agreed to purchase a box, all the while warning me she was doubtful I'd be boating that weekend. She bought a box of Tampax that very afternoon and I studied her as she read the box, the brochure inside, and she even opened a packet to scrutinize the product. I could tell by the look on her face she'd found no evidence I would die or go to hell using a different type of protection for one single day.

"Well, you'd best take these instructions into the bathroom with you and give this a trial run." Her voice wasn't a happy one, but I felt things were looking up.

Once inside the bathroom, I read everything printed on the box, and then delved into the brochure and diagrams. *Whoa . . . this looks more complicated than I expected,* I thought to myself. Unwrapping the tampon gave me pause again— cardboard! The applicator felt exactly like a lightweight version of cardboard, or maybe a heavy-duty paper plate. To top things off, the applicator tube's end had an edge that was less than soft and smooth.

My first attempt was a miserable failure. Not only did the insertion go awry, the stupid applicator fell right into the toilet. It looked like a small submarine that had just surfaced from somewhere deep in the sewer system! I giggled. Using one of Mom's hairpins, I snagged the sopping wet applicator and wrapped the useless item in tissue, tossing it into the trash.

My second attempt seemed to go well, even though I can't say it was comfortable. That blunt edge felt like a solid ring of tiny scalpels scraping away at delicate tissue while being inserted. *What idiot designed this thing? Must've been a man,* I thought.

I found Mom sitting in the kitchen, sipping coffee and tapping her toe while she awaited my report.

"OK, so I wouldn't want to use tampons all of the time, but for a day on the lake, I'll be fine," I announced. The look of concern was still on her face, although she didn't say a word.

I grabbed a Coke from the fridge, plopped down on the couch to watch television, and immediately levitated back to a standing position. *What the . . . ?* I felt like I had just been impaled by an upright corn cob! Something was NOT right.

I hightailed it back into the bathroom and removed the tampon, which had somehow managed to slip halfway out by itself. The product had to be faulty—surely it wasn't a failure on my part to understand instructions.

That night, I tried on my black bathing suit and a pad, which was hitched up to one of those disgusting belts. *Oh yeah, major belt lines!* However, the snug, elasticized, black suit did a fine job of keeping the pad in place. My mind was made up— I'd skip the belt, and to hide the pad, I'd keep a towel wrapped around my waist at all times, except when I was in the water. And Mom could just assume I was the Tampon Queen, for I would never admit failure—and I was going skiing! It was my favorite sport and no monthly curse was going to stop me.

Saturday came and my first skiing stint went perfectly. When I ran out of steam, I let go of the rope and sank slowly into the water. While the boat circled around to pick me up, I did an underwater pad check—it was still there. *Woo, hoo!* The moment I was back onboard, I wrapped the towel—sarong style—around my waist.

I rested while the guys skied, and then hopped into the water for another round of jumping wakes like a champ. Soon into my run, a large boat charged across the lake like it was on fire and came a little too close. Talk about wakes! It was more like tsunami time—when the first monstrous wave hit me, I crashed so hard it felt as if I hit concrete.

This time, as the boat circled around to pick me up, I spied my pad floating on top of the water! If they had already designed pads with wings it would have looked just like an albino fish, with strange looking fins. I grabbed that thing and held it underwater, hoping it would absorb enough water to sink. Each time I let go, it bobbed to the top again. I crammed it partially under the elastic around one of the leg openings of my swimsuit and waited for the boat. Just as I was about to climb aboard, I shoved the pad under the boat, with a wish that it stay put until we took off, and it did! Panicked, I wrapped the towel around me in record time; I was like a sitting duck during hunting season—I had no protection at all.

While cruising around, I'd occasionally hang my sarong over the side, swish it out, and rewrap, always fussing about how hot I was. My exciting day had turned into a day from hell. I decided becoming a woman was not the thrill I'd expected—it was for the birds, not for fun!

Just before heading in to load the boat, my brother and I decided to ski together, the only thing we'd not done the entire day. We'd also planned to ski in close to the shoreline and walk out of the lake. It was always a challenge to see how close to the shore we could get. Sometimes we'd sink before we expected and had to swim to shore, while other times we got so close we could step out of our skis and actually walk onto solid ground near the loading ramp. Then, by the time the boat arrived, we would be waiting to help load it onto the trailer.

As we neared the docks and ramp area, we dropped our ski ropes and were on our way. I hadn't judged my speed or location worth a damn. I saw disaster looming, but had no control over it. I remember the sound of both ski tips smashing into the barrels under someone's dock—and then me lying flat on my back on the dock! I did hear one of the guys say, "Get the tool box out of the trunk—NOW!" I was fuzzy and disoriented, but knew they sounded serious.

I'd slammed into the barrels with enough force that one of the open-toed bindings was now around my upper thigh with the ski still attached—resting beneath my body. I didn't feel a thing as the guys worked frantically to free me from the ski. However, I was aware I'd chipped a lower tooth.

The minute I truly came to my senses, I demanded my sarong! No, I had not forgotten my precarious condition. I covered myself, but remained flat on my back while they loaded the boat onto the trailer. Barreling into barrels had taken quite a toll, and I felt far from hale and hearty.

"Don't try to get up! We'll carry you to the car," my brother said. Both guys grabbed an arm and pulled me into a sitting position. I was slightly dizzy, but told them to get on with things. I just wanted to get home.

I wrapped one arm around my brother's neck and with his arms under my knees we struck out for the car. "Look!" shouted his best pal, pointing at a pool of blood on the dock. "I didn't see any gashes, but Kathy is bleeding somewhere. We've got to hurry—she may need to go to the hospital. What if she's got an internal injury that's bleeding? She could die!"

I wanted to shoot him. *Internal injury—no! Bleeding internally—BINGO!*

Our very alert family friend followed us to the car, announcing on several occasions, "Oh no, there's another drop of blood!"

Just great, I thought to myself. *I'm leaving a trail of blood splats for the world to see.* Yeah, becoming a woman is grand. I'd only wanted a day on the lake. Instead, I had nearly killed myself, and the guys all but had me on my death bed.

"Oh, it's probably just a little scrape somewhere. Toss a towel on the car seat, I'll be fine," I instructed.

We headed for home at breakneck speed. After being asked numerous times to poke about on my abdomen for tender spots, I told them to leave me alone and wake me when we got home. I feigned sleep, listening to the guys yammer on about my condition. They all but planned my funeral. At first I stifled chuckles. However, their concern was so sincere that as time passed, I did consider blurting out the truth.

With each mile we drove, more sensation began returning to my foot, calf and thigh; my leg looked as if someone had tried to skin me alive. The bindings had not given an inch, but the skin on my leg certainly did. Otherwise, I'd likely have had some broken bones. Each time I snuck a peek, my leg was a deeper shade of purple. By the time we arrived home, I was in agony and looked like I'd been in a car wreck.

Mom heard us pull into the gravel driveway. She opened the door to find me in my brother's arms, wrapped like a mummy in blood-stained towels with a purple leg dangling from beneath another beach towel. Every smidgen of color drained from her face.

"Mom, I'm all right, really I am! A few scrapes here and there, otherwise I'm fine. Don't worry."

Both guys began to jabber about the accident, my mysterious bleeding issue and stated that I probably needed an ambulance. Mom's eyes darted from them to me. She was terrified.

"Just carry me into the bathroom before I get blood on the carpet," I ordered my brother. "I'll tell Mom what hap-

pened. Go put the boat away. You're just making her nervous."
I was so snippy, he should probably have just dropped me onto
the floor!

Mom and I convened behind the closed bathroom door.
She was frazzled as she began her inspection, starting with my
battered leg. Knowing she'd never find a bleeding gash and not
wanting to be rushed to the hospital, I came clean about my
tampon failure. I felt like a heathen. Mom's face changed in a
moment—I'd never seen such relief wash over anyone in my
entire life, ever. I apologized for misleading her. She smiled as
she cleaned my wounds.

Actually, relief washed over the both of us. I had not told
the truth in the beginning, and the consequence was evident.
And as with anybody, guilt has knocked loudly a few more
times in my life and has been a visitor I loathed. But not as
much as my monthly cycle. Thank God for menopause!

Piano Blues

by
Beverly Higginson

With less than six months of lessons under our belts, my big sister and I played in our first piano recital. It was held in a high-school auditorium. Two grand pianos were positioned on opposite sides of the stage, and each of us pupils—10 in all—took the stage when it was our turn to play. The audience sat mostly in dim light, which was OK with me. We novice plunkers could barely see their faces.

At that particular time in my life, piano was not my choice of artistic expression. My best friend had just started taking dance lessons and had come by the house with her shiny patent-leather tap shoes. She insisted I try them on, and wouldn't you know it, they were a perfect fit. She watched me click and clack along our front walkway. She even taught me the time step. I was captivated.

"Please," I begged my mother, "please let me take tap lessons." But my mother was more interested in manners and appearances. She blew me off. Piano playing, she explained, especially of the classics, indicated good taste and refinement, whereas tap dancing did not. I broke into a demonstration of the time-step, but she wasn't impressed. Since I was barely nine years old, I didn't have much chance debating taste and refinement with my mother. Case closed.

My mother hired a piano instructor who came highly recommended, though we never knew how she found the guy. He had a broad square face, always wore the same rumpled black suit, and carried a fedora. However strange he was, his primary appeal to my mother was that he came to us to teach. The lessons would be given in our very own living room on a slightly-used upright piano Mom had talked Dad into buying. The piano arrived one day in a truck that rolled right through our neighborhood baseball game, coming to a stop in front of my house. When the smoke cleared, the empty space in our living room was filled with a piano and I was signed up for lessons.

My sister proved the better pianist. I had to practice harder, which I hated. But I managed to learn my recital piece—*Sonatina*—backward and forward. Well, maybe not backward, but really well. I surprised myself because one, I really liked *Sonatina*, and two, that first recital turned out great. I didn't make one mistake. But that didn't mean I was anxious for a repeat performance.

So what happened next? The maestro told us he had arranged a second recital the following week. He called it a "tea" that would be held at an estate home, and he wanted his best pupils to perform. That included my sister and me.

There we were on Sunday at this fancy house dressed in our church-going best. A large enclosed patio was decorated with flowers. Folding chairs were set up for the audience, and a slightly-elevated platform with a baby grand piano was in place for the performance.

The room filled quickly. Mom, Dad, my younger sister, my visiting grandmother and our piano-loving neighbors filed into the third row and took their seats. Five of us pupils were already on the stage watching the seats fill. We were trapped. I looked to my sister for reassurance, but she was looking straight ahead, her eyes kind of squinty. Her hands were folded neatly in her lap, and in a strange voice she said, "I don't want to play today."

"What?" I said, almost shouting.

In her sudden annoyance at having to perform, she left her seat and approached the maestro and told him she did not want to play and he couldn't make her. You would have thought she stuck him in the rear with a needle the way his eyes shot open. Through very tight lips, he persuaded her to retake her seat.

While the first pupil played, my sister whispered to me that she would cut the middle section of her piece and no one would know the difference.

Performing second on the program, she took her seat at the piano and proceeded to do exactly what she promised. She played only the beginning and the ending. I knew, because I had heard her play that piece a hundred times. She left out a big hunk of it. When she was done, my sister bowed at the waist and smirked triumphantly at me as she took her seat.

Such a force was my sister that the minute she decided she didn't want to play, I didn't want to play, either. Why was I on the spot again, getting all worked up and nervous? *I don't want to play.* I didn't say it out loud, but a voice inside my head was shrieking. The more I thought about it, the more agitated I became. I wanted to jump up and run. But I couldn't.

My turn was next. *OK,* I thought. *I know what to do. I'd do what my sister did. If she could cut her piece short, so could I. I'd abbreviate the old* Sonatina *and be done with it.*

As I seated myself on the bench, the music swirled in my head and, at the same time, I tried to keep my knees from knocking together. I didn't dare look at the audience or the maestro. *Only look at the keys.* I placed my fingers on them, pressed the introductory two notes, and then NOTHING. My fingers locked. Or maybe it was my brain that locked. I shook out my hands and began again. But again they froze, right along with my head. I couldn't remember what came after the first two notes. Over and over I kept hitting those first two notes, but the more I tried to go forward, the worse it got.

Suddenly, I could hear my own breathing, like rushing water, and then panting. I squirmed on the bench, leaned in over the keys and willed my fingers to continue, but they splayed like tentacles. And then the keys started blurring and shimmering, melting together, white into black, fuzzy like in a kaleidoscope. I blinked down at the blur. *Where the heck is middle C?*

The audience was so quiet. Not knowing what to do, I stood up. Everyone was looking at me. I sucked in a huge gasp of air and wailed, "I want my daddy!"

Hey, I was nine.

I sprinted down the aisle and fell into my dad's arms. I felt Grandma's comforting pats on my back and glimpsed at Mom, who was looking off like she didn't know me. To her, the moment definitely lacked refinement. From the audience came a smattering of applause and a sympathetic "aaahh." I closed my eyes, wishing I could disappear.

On the ride home, my sister gave me weird looks. "You know that dippy piece like your own name. What happened?" I would never tell her I was trying to duplicate her keyboard slight-of-hand, and that by trying to sabotage *Sonatina*, I had sabotaged myself.

I simply went with Mom's explanation. "Just a bad case of stage fright," she said. "You'll do better next time."

But my sister had me figured out. "You can't do what I do," she whispered.

Over the next few years, I played in several more recitals and managed not to embarrass myself. I recognized early on that becoming a concert pianist was probably not in my future. But I performed well. No shenanigans and no attempts at shortcuts. I had come to love classical music, and when I played, my mother beamed. Mission accomplished.

In more ways than one, I had learned my lesson.

Winter Escapade

by
Marilyn Acker

"Let's do it," all of us agreed.

"But what if we get caught?" I worried out loud, having second thoughts.

"There's no way. We'll be back by the time school lets out and home at our usual time," Esther raised her eyebrows and spread her hands out while cajoling me.

Esther was the oldest of our group and lived with her dad. He had bought her a 1953 Ford Sunliner convertible, while the rest of us didn't even have our driver's licenses yet. She was also the wildest. That's why we liked her.

Diane suggested with wide eyes, "Oooh, we could cross the bridge and go into St. Louis. You know that cool skating rink in Pinelawn that plays live organ music? Let's go there!" She scooted her feet one at a time with her hands on her hips.

"Yeah, and we could go to Steak 'n Shake on Rock Road and have burgers and shakes," Carolyn's voice rose as she got into it.

"Wow, I don't know. My parents would kill me. I've never skipped school before," I said, still unsure.

"None of us has, except for Esther," Diane assured me. "There's just no way we could get caught. And we'll write each other a parent's note saying we were sick. We're all in different classes, so no one will suspect a thing."

An only child, I was smart enough not to pull too many tricks. As I always said, I got the best and the worst of childhood. I couldn't blame anything on siblings. I thought about it for a minute. Riding in a convertible with the top down in March—the four of us cruising around St. Louis like we were older than our mere 15 years—sounded like a great time. Esther knew how to have fun, and I wanted in on some of it.

"OK, I'm in!" I shouted, grinning.

Esther picked the three of us up for school the next morning as usual. Heading across the bridge, we were laughing and singing. Stopping at the first donut shop we came to, Esther put the convertible top down and ordered breakfast. She then rolled up the convertible windows and turned on the heater to high. A little cold weather wasn't going to stop us.

It would be nice if the sun would come out, I thought, as I sat shivering.

We went to the zoo and walked around, acting silly and giggly, flirting with the guys working at the food court, swinging our poodle skirts and layers of petticoats, coats unbuttoned. I had my new rabbit fur collar hooked on my sweater which helped with the cold. Esther sashayed up to one hunky guy selling cotton candy, and by the smile on his face, we knew she had him hooked. I dragged her away, and we headed for the car.

After a Steak 'n Shake lunch, we drove to the skating rink. *Blue Suede Shoes* was blaring from the car radio while we cruised down the highway, singing at the top of our voices, hair blowing free in the wind.

We rented skates and twirled to *Love Me Tender*, swooning to Elvis and checking out older guys on the floor. The organ player wasn't there on a weekday, but the music was still good. Laughing, we pushed the door to leave and stopped suddenly. The open convertible was covered in snow—the seats, the dashboard, the windows. It had to have been 3 inches deep and was still coming down hard.

"No! What are we going to do?" I squealed. Everyone was talking and screeching at once.

"My dad's going to be furious!" Esther cried out. "Look at my car!"

Diane, the brainy one, went into the skating rink and borrowed some towels. Our hands were red and frozen and our shoes ruined by the time we had the snow brushed out. Esther got the car started, put the top up and blasted the heater. All of us were wet, cold and scared.

Driving the back roads home to avoid the main highway, the convertible's wheels lost traction and slipped going up the smallest inclines. And because our brakes were useless on the slick roads, we slid through several red lights. We crawled along until we came to an intersection that had a hill where cars were sliding all over.

"Do you think we can make it home before school is out?" I whined.

"Heck, I think they probably let school out early," Carolyn

stated, with fear in her voice.

"OHMYGOSH, we are in big trouble!" I cried. My dad was at home from work this week, and I had never defied him. I was devastated with worry. The other girls didn't seem too concerned as they had pretty lenient parents.

Esther stepped on the gas to make the hill, but our car slid toward the ditch and got stuck in a snow bank. The three of us climbed out of the car and, in our good Sears clothes and coats, pushed the convertible. I was behind the driver's-side back wheel, and slush flew up all over me. I kept pushing and crying and pushing. Finally, the wheels got a grip and tore forward. Carolyn, Diane and I fell to the ground. Esther drove to a patch of pavement and stopped.

"We did it!" we all shouted as we jumped back in the car. Covered in dirty wet snow and feeling miserable, we were on our way. We crept across the bridge toward home.

"Let's pray our parents will feel so sorry for us and be so grateful we made it back safe, they won't be mad," Carolyn whimpered. I looked over at her and her hair was frozen to her forehead.

Esther dropped Diane off first—her mother stood at the door shaking her head. Carolyn, Esther and I lived in the same subdivision, so Esther dropped us off at the end of our street and headed on home. I walked into the house, nervous and fearful. Mom and Dad, with worried faces, sat at the kitchen table drinking coffee. I started crying.

"I guess you know what happened?" I asked with tears streaking down my face.

Dad didn't say anything for a couple of minutes. Mom left the room. "When it started snowing, I saw neighbor kids coming home from school. You didn't come home, so I called Esther's dad to make sure there wasn't an accident. It was easy then to figure out what you girls had done," Dad said, with a disappointed look. "Your mother and I decided you've already been punished enough. However, we are grounding you from Esther's convertible for two months."

Despite the fear we had shared trying to get home that night, at school the next day we bragged to everyone about our big adventure across the bridge. And even though we regretted putting our parents through all that worry, it didn't stop us from doing it two more times before we graduated. We just didn't get quite as adventurous or go quite so far from home, and we checked the weather forecast first. My parents had it pretty easy with me for the most part—I rarely got grounded for anything.

The irony of it all was that when Dad was in his 80s and came to live with me, he would bring up the awful thing I had done by skipping school that snowy day, and he would tell my grown kids what a handful I had been. If only he knew what kids were doing these days!

Carolyn, Marilyn and Diane

How *Not* to Get to Second Base

by
Kevin Kane

For the first 12 years of my life, I enjoyed a typical nuclear family: two parents, a sister, a house in the suburbs and a dog named Fluffy. Seriously. At some point just prior to when I turned 13, a family reactor apparently lost cooling power and there was a meltdown, the upshot of which was my parents sought a divorce and I, wise beyond my years, elected to move out and live with my father.

Dad was a successful attorney, but not the type who worked crazy hours. But he was also newly single, in his early 40s, and ready to hit the 1980s' dating scene head on. Picture, if you will, the gold chain, gold Rolex and Porsche 911 convertible. Dad had it all. Dad was a cliché. So while Dad was working and getting his groove on, I was attending school and, um, growing up. Fast. When I was 15, Dad trusted me, but let it be known that he would give me enough rope to either run free and enjoy it or get tangled. "Don't hang yourself, Kevin," Dad would warn.

When you are done with school at 3 P.M. but do not have adult supervision until 6:30 P.M., there is plenty of time for homework, laundry, cutting the lawn and finding Dad's poorly hidden adult videos. Once primed with the knowledge of how things operated between men and women, albeit in a very graphic and poorly-acted fashion, I sought out my "Ginger" or "Honey" with whom I could try these neat new tricks. Unfortunately, no 15-year-old girl was about to get into a cab and come over to my house—and no mother was going to allow her daughter to come over to the notorious Kane household where adult supervision was fleeting.

Lucky for me, my father always impressed upon me the value of solving problems. He wanted me to be able to recognize problems, study and appreciate my options, and then, once the options were considered, make a rational and reasoned decision on how to solve the problem in the most efficient manner. For example, if you have a girlfriend who wants to come over to hang out—and I did—but she cannot take a cab or get dropped off by a parent, you must figure out how to get said girlfriend to your house by other means. So, employing the tools honed by my father and passed to me, I recognized that there was an extra car in our garage most days, that the keys to the car were hanging next to the door to the garage, and that I, the master of driving our lawn-mowing tractor, could easily drive a car.

My first excursions in Dad's doo-doo brown, 1980 Chevy Caprice involved quick laps around the neighborhood. Since we had moved there only a year or so before I began my joy rides, we did not really know our neighbors and, fortunately, they did not know us. That eliminated the risk of a nosy neighbor busting me for driving without a license. There was virtually no risk of trouble, assuming I did not draw attention to myself and the four-door turd that I captained.

Pretty soon, the neighborhood lost its luster and I needed more open roads. I craved the speed of larger roads, the test of properly timing my launch from a stoplight, and learning how to get to my new girlfriend's house. Of course, venturing out included the risk of one of Dad's friends seeing me or his extra car and busting me, but, hey, I really wanted to get past second base.

One day, Dad announced that he and his girlfriend were going away for the night to somewhere in the Virginia countryside. It was a Friday night and Georgetown in Washington, D.C. would be party central. I feigned disappointment and asked all the prudent questions: Where are you going? How far away is it? What time will you be back? Each question was framed to determine how much time I had to get to Georgetown and back without the risk of getting busted. Dad thought I was being responsible. I was, just not in the way he thought I was. Off went Dad and the girlfriend, leaving me, his über responsible and trustworthy 15-year-old son, at home for the night. Cue the *Risky Business* sound track.

I called my girlfriend, who also lived in a single-parent home and was likewise afforded more freedoms than nuclear-family kids. I told her to put on a dress and get ready to head to Georgetown with me. I pulled on my Guess jeans, moussed my hair, slathered on the Drakkar Noir, and headed for the car. My girl was ready when I arrived; things were going perfectly! Together we cruised from the Bethesda, Maryland suburbs into Georgetown, radio blaring, with not a care in the world. It was Friday night—we were headed to Georgetown, and were, at that moment, the coolest kids on the planet.

The parking situation in Georgetown was tighter than a frog's anus. I had circled the block several times and came to an intersection where I decided to make a U-turn. Bad call. You see, the traffic cops in Georgetown were notoriously grumpy and very quick to blip their sirens, light up the emergency lights and pull over anyone who dared to even appear to violate the most minor traffic law.

After completing my beautifully executed U-turn, Officer Sullivan, or O'Callahan, or some other stereotypical Irish cop straight out of Central Casting, lit up the lights, pinged the siren and screamed at me over the loudspeaker to "PULL OVER!" *Crap*. Literally. I was about to crap in my pants. Being the responsible young lad that I was, I immediately pulled over. Running was not an option. My girlfriend was too slow—too slow of a runner, that is. It seemed to take forever for the cop to approach the car and the tension in the Brown Bomber was palpable. My girl asked me what we were going to do. I told her I did not know. I remember thinking to myself, *Problem solve, damn it. C'mon, Kevin. You've got this.*

When Officer O'Reilly (not his real name) walked up to my window, I was facing a middle-aged, overweight and under-compensated police officer who had the unfortunate task of pulling traffic duty in Georgetown on a Friday night. He barked at me to hand him my license and registration. I told a little white lie and informed the policeman that everything was in the car's glove compartment. Knowing that my father was a seasoned pack rat, I was hoping that the glove box was stuffed to the brim with all manner of papers. Dad did not disappoint. When the door to the glove compartment fell open, papers exploded, creating a torrent of cellulose, ice scrapers, old parking tickets and loose change.

As I slowly picked through the papers, Barney Fife got annoyed and told me to bring my license and registration back to the police car when I found them. I continued my doomed search just for appearances. Knowing I faced certain defeat, I grabbed the vehicle registration and did the walk of shame back to the police car. No amount of childhood trouble and facing punishment from my parents ever prepared me for this confrontation. I was screwed and I knew it.

I handed the cop the registration and told my second white lie of the night: "I could not find my license."

Clearly annoyed, Officer Sheamus O'Connor (not his real name) asked me point blank, "Don't bullshit me, kid. Do you have a license or not?" In the most humbled, terrified voice I could muster, I eschewed any further obfuscation and owned up to my illegal status. I anticipated the very next words out of his mouth, but was surprised by what followed.

"Step away from the car and have a seat on the curb," ordered my furious new surrogate parent. I was busted, terrified and definitely not getting past second base tonight. I took a seat on the cold cement curb and awaited additional instructions.

My captor continued doing something in the police car,

eventually emerging with a stern look and a purposeful gait that had a slight hitch, undoubtedly due to chafing from his polyester uniform pants. After staring me down for what seemed like an eternity, the officer began, "Let me get this straight, Mr. Kane. You thought you would hop into your parents' car, pick up your little girlfriend over there, and head to Georgetown for a good time. Is that it?"

Suppressing every smart-ass impulse to congratulate my genius captor for mastering the obvious, I pinched my leg, forced out a tear for effect and responded in the affirmative.

Seizing upon my perceived vulnerability, brought about by my lone prop of a tear, he continued, "You know that I can bring you downtown and have you locked up?" The next rhetorical question was my favorite. "Do you know how all the fellas in lock-up would love to share a cell with a handsome little white kid like you?" Cue more forced tears to sate the cop's sadistic side. I nodded vigorously to show my fear.

The rant continued, "You're scared right now, aren't you."

Palm to my forehead with a sarcastic "No shit? Really?" look on my face would have been perfectly appropriate here, but would have probably ruined the mileage I had gained with the tears and submissive nodding.

"Yes, sir," I immediately agreed, with my voice cracking and loud, irregular breathing thrown in for effect. Then came the curveball I never expected.

"Tonight's your lucky night, Mr. Kane,"

HUH??? WHAT???

"I'm putting the Block Rule in place. You know what that means?"

Um, no since it's a figment of your feeble imagination. "No, sir," I answered sheepishly, instead.

"Well, it goes something like this: you get yourself home, your little girlie there home, and the car home without coming within a block of that vehicle," he emphasized by pointing to the turd mobile, "and we're gonna forget all about this little situation."

But the cop was not yet done with me. "And if you fail to follow my instructions, I WILL take you downtown, and I WILL throw you in the holding cell with all the fellas, and you WILL experience something no one your age should ever feel. Got it?"

"Yes. Yes, of course!" I responded like a woman responding to a marriage proposal. Swish, swish went Barney Fife's pants as he walked off into the sunset. I pretended to pray so Barney would take greater pleasure in his perceived act of mercy. Then the lights on the police car went dark, the cop drove off and I was left sitting there with a shit-eating grin and a rather large dent in my halo.

I now had the Herculean task of complying with the mysterious Block Rule. Equally important to getting home was doing so without anyone—namely, Dad—finding out.

Thinking cap on, problem solving initiated. Here were the factors: I needed two people to help me, both with driver's licenses. I needed two since they would have to drive together down to Georgetown, and one of them would then drive the Brown Bomber home for me. I had to get my girlfriend home as well, but I had not yet given up hope on passing second base with her. After all, I fought the law and won. Surely that should at least get a guy a handful of boobs, no? Finally, I had to make sure that Dad did not find out. Tow truck? Too expensive. Leave the car there and cab it home and return tomorrow with Dad? Too expensive in another way. And then it hit me. The greatest thought I have ever summoned. Call my math tutor and his brother, both legally licensed and good people.

Even though it was Friday night, I was pretty sure Jeff and Don would be home. They were 17, straight-A students, members of the cross-country team, and more likely to be tearing apart a video game than tearing open a beer. I found a nearby pay phone and called. "Hi, Jeff. It's Kevin." Surprised to hear my voice, Jeff acknowledged me, and we traded some small talk about football, school, that kind of thing. Then I went in for the favor.

"Jeff, I'm kind of in a situation. I would be eternally grateful if you and Don would drive to Georgetown and give me a ride home. It's a long story and you cannot tell your parents that you are coming to get me. Can you help me out?"

And then came the second greatest words of the night after Barney Fife's words of freedom. "Yes, of course." *Wow, I just might pull this off.*

My girlfriend had gotten over her earlier fear and anger and was now in adventure mode with me. She liked the thrill of the hunt. She had nice boobs. I explained to her my plan and how it would work. "So we're not going to the bars?"

Mammary massaging hopes dashed, I broke the news to her. "We're lucky not to be in jail! Let's go home and forget about tonight."

About 30 minutes later, Jeff and Don rolled up Prospect Street in Georgetown. I asked Don to drive home the Brown

Bomber while my now dejected girl and I rode with Jeff in his car.

I explained the entire evening to Jeff as we drove home. He was incredulous. I was an idiot—but an adventurous idiot. We dropped my girl at her house, and although I got a kiss for my troubles, I got nothing more. Jeff, my savior, was evidently also a cock-blocker.

We met Don at my house where he repositioned the Bomber into the comfy confines of the garage, exactly where the night had begun. I thanked them profusely, offered them a case of Dad's beer, and pledged to them my first-born son in exchange for their assistance and eternal confidentiality. I walked inside, drank a beer and passed out.

Upon his return from his overnight trip, Dad was none the wiser about my adventure the previous night. And he stayed that way, thanks to my friends. In fact, I do not think that I told Dad about that night until Visiting Day my junior year of college, right after I sold the motorcycle he also knew nothing about.

Scandalous

by
Ireta Black

Believe it or not, peer pressure is timeless. It got the best of me in 1933, which got me in a lot of trouble, too.

I was only 10 years old when I decided, like many of the other kids, I just *had* to wear ankle socks to school. It was as simple as that. But Momma and Daddy wouldn't let me because they thought a young girl showing too much leg was indecent. Instead, I had to wear old-fashioned socks that went all the way up to my knees. Those old socks were OK in the winter because back then, girls wore dresses most of the time. A Kansas winter could chill you right to the bone and back again.

My cousin Reba lived right behind us. We were the same age and went to the same school. Her mom wasn't as strict as my parents and Reba got to wear what she wanted, within reason, and do whatever she wanted. And oh, did she have some beautiful ankle socks! I would drool over them when we walked to school together. I wanted a pair so badly myself.

What made things worse was that the other girls at school also wore ankle socks. They teased me over my knee-high socks and weren't very kind. I was so desperate to fit in that I would roll my long socks down as far as they would go when I got to school, and then roll them back up on the way home.

One spring day, both Reba and I were invited to a class-mate's birthday party. It was the talk of the school, and all of us 10-year-old girls were excited to go. But deep down inside, I fretted because I knew I would be the only girl at the party not wearing ankle socks. I shared my fear with Reba.

"Oh, don't you worry none, Ireta. I've got an idea," Reba said, with a sparkle in her eye. She knew I was a worrywart.

On the day of the party, Reba told me to come to her house and pick her up. When I got there, she slipped some-thing into the pocket of my party dress. It was a pair of ankle socks! I gasped then smiled. *What would Momma do if she knew?* I worried to myself as we walked to the party.

But the worry quickly turned to delight. Far enough away from our homes, I sat down and took off my old socks. I then slowly, and with great anticipation, pulled the beautiful white socks on. Slipping back into my shoes, I stood up. I felt like a princess! I pranced and twirled and admired the socks. Then I gave Reba a big hug.

"Thank you so much! I love them!" I said to her.

"You're welcome. But know they're my best ones and I'm just letting you borrow them for the party, OK?" Reba said. I agreed and shoved my old socks into my pocket.

The party was grand and I felt like the cat's meow in my

pretty ankle socks. I floated from group to group, making sure everyone saw I was wearing them. No one teased me. No one smirked at me. I had finally become one of the crowd.

When we left the party, I switched socks again and put the ankle socks in my pocket. I was so happy that when I waved goodbye to Reba, I forgot to give them back to her. Momma had a whole list of chores for me to do as soon as I got home; I went upstairs and changed out of my party clothes and got busy on the list.

The next day, Momma was out in the yard, standing over our small outdoor fire pit. She had a long stick and was stoking the fire.

"Whatcha doing, Momma?" I asked her as I walked up from behind.

"Burnin' your ankle socks."

It took a moment for me to digest what she had just said. Then it hit me—she was burning Reba's prized socks!

"No, Momma, stop! They're . . . " then I caught myself because I didn't want to blab on Reba and get both of us in trouble. One of us in trouble was enough.

From that day on, Momma watched my every move. While I had disobeyed her and Daddy, a little part of me didn't feel too bad about being naughty, because, for one day, I felt like the belle of the ball. And Reba eventually forgave me, but she never lent me anything ever again!

Night of Crime

by
Bobby Barbara Smith

I grew up in a rural farm community, where old customs and traditions lingered far longer than in suburban and city areas. I attended a one-room school house that housed first through eighth grades, and all were taught by a single teacher. The stone building had a basement, which was used for pie suppers, school plays, Christmas programs and Halloween costume parties. I loved it all, but especially the event that resulted in a personal discovery—the night my first-ever crime took place.

It happened when I was in fifth grade. The school was buzzing with plans for the Halloween costume party. There would be apple bobbing, decorations, prizes for the best costumes. And this year, they added a new category—anyone who could keep their identity a secret the whole evening would win a prize!

We were poor. There was precious little money and certainly

none for such foolishness, but Mother was an excellent seamstress with a great imagination. She always managed to come up with creative costumes. This year I was to be a clown, and we had a clown face left over from my older siblings, the kind with the eye and mouth holes and the black elastic string to secure it to your head. Mother set about sewing colorful scraps of fabric on muslin, and in no time I had a clown suit. She then took a mophead, dyed it yellow, trimmed it up and it became my hair.

But what was I to do about my shoes? Everyone would guess who I was by my shoes! Alas, I was doomed to be recognized. I should not have doubted Mother's ingenuity, however. She went to the closet and brought out my brother's old lace-up work shoes. He'd long outgrown them, and they were very ragged—perfect for a clown. She stuffed the toes with rags so that my small feet wouldn't flop around, laced them tight around the clown suit, and *voilà*! My clown costume was complete. *No one would ever discover my identity now,* I thought to myself.

I thought that evening would never come. I would be on my own, since my siblings had graduated, but I didn't care. When it was finally time for the party, Dad dropped me off, and as I made my way to the basement door, a group of older boys rushed toward me.

I should point out that I was not part of the popular kids' clique, and so to find myself surrounded by the older, popular seventh- and eighth-grade boys was alarming!

"Hey, Danny," I recognized the voice of an upper classman, but held my breath, "Great costume! You look great!"

He slapped me on the shoulder, and I nearly lost my balance.

Oh no! I thought, *they think I'm one of their friends!* My mind raced as I tried to figure out how to convince them I wasn't Danny. I wasn't even a boy! I mustered up my gruffest mysterious voice.

"I'm not Danny," I growled, which brought cheers and laughter from them all.

"Yeah, sure, we know it's you. Come on. We won't tell anyone." They walked with me, as I tried to make my way to the door.

The more I insisted, the louder they laughed, and then I heard the words that struck terror in my heart.

"OK, Mr.-Clown-who's-not-Danny, we don't care who you are, but we need you to help us turn over the girls' outhouse." The older boy threw his arm around my shoulder and started walking me down the path toward the target.

I didn't know what to do. I dared not reveal my identity! They had shared their evil plan with me, and I was now guilty by association. My heart was beating out of my chest as they discussed how to accomplish the prank. I was frozen in place, with the angry face of my teacher flashing before me. And, oh, dear God, my mother was going to kill me!

"Come on, Danny, what's wrong with you? You act like you've never done this before!" The older boy shoved me toward the pile of pushing boys, and I was thinking I could really use this bathroom right now. But instead of using the facilities, I grabbed a corner and pretended to push. Suddenly, the dirty deed was done, and the smell was horrible! I couldn't make my way back up that path quickly enough, and the older classmates were hurrying also, not wanting to get caught in the area.

As we all arrived at the head of the path, they were giggling like a bunch of girls, but scattered as a truck pulled into the parking lot. Another clown got out of the truck. *Danny!* My heart leapt into my throat as I scooted inside the door, but not before I heard Danny's voice and a flurry of excitement coming from the older boys.

I no longer cared about the prize. I was most assuredly going to jail, and then straight to hell. I found an empty chair between two rather large women and slinked down in the seat, praying for the night to be over.

The evening dragged while I prayed God would take me home—either home to my mother or to Heaven—it didn't matter, anywhere but here. The event finally wound down, and my teacher walked to the front of the room. I knew the time had come to award the coveted prize, and I feared what would happen once the boys found out who I was. I could feel their eyes staring at the back of my head, but I dared not turn around for even a peek.

Just then one of the mothers made her way up to the teacher and whispered something in his ear. His face turned beet red, and I knew our crime had been discovered. I peered over the seat and relief washed over me when I saw Dad standing in the doorway. I rushed to his side as our teacher announced, in a loud and angry voice, that the girls' outhouse had been vandalized, and our evening would have to end, thanks to the bad behavior of a few rotten apples.

Dad turned and headed for the truck, and as I followed, I heard the teacher speaking in a loud voice. "The following boys will stay behind and help upright the girl's outhouse and clean up the mess." He was calling the names of every older boy who had pushed over the outhouse. How did he know? As I climbed into the truck I heard one last name called—Danny's.

It wasn't until we were halfway home that I dared to relax, and then a smile slid across my face, and a giggle burst out of me.

"You say something?" Dad cast a look my way.

"No, just clearing my throat," I lied, adding to the pile of sins weighing heavily on my shoulders. I stifled any further giggling, but could not wipe the smile off my face.

The remaining days of my fifth-grade year flew by, and although my days returned to normal—with the older students unaware of my existence—I would watch those boys gather on the playground, and I would recall that exciting evening when I was part of their little huddle. I never spoke a word about my involvement that night, not even to my best friend. It was too delicious, it made me feel perfectly wicked, and sharing would somehow spoil it. No, this was a secret I'd take to my grave— those boys will never know the true identity of the clown who aided their criminal activity that night, until now!

Bobby and her school, which is now a community center.

The Mystery of the Gridiron Chalk Phallus

by
Brent Goldstein

There is an art to a good adolescent prank. A truly successful prank usually requires a deft combination of many factors, including timing, creativity, audacity, spontaneity, execution, reaction and, yes, often some alcohol-fueled stupidity.

I attended Wootton High School in Rockville, Maryland. I played on the golf team, but most of my friends were football players. Back then, most high school football games were played on Saturday afternoons. This meant that Friday nights I was often left to my own devices due to coach-imposed Friday night pre-game curfews on the football team. However, once every season, Wootton played football on a Friday night and those were special occasions, not just because of the rare thrill of playing (and watching) a game under the bright lights, but because once the game ended, my football friends were free from Friday-night curfews.

After one particular Friday night game in October 1984, I was hanging out after the game with five or six of my buddies from the football team, trying in vain to think of something to do. Unfortunately, entertainment options for teenagers in the 'burbs were pretty limited after 10 P.M. Typically, nights like this ended with a bunch of us drinking beer on a secluded street, cranking Led Zeppelin albums from a boom-box.

This night was no different. (Yes, we were losers!) Around 2 A.M., and after strumming the air-guitar to *Communication Breakdown* for the third time, someone mentioned that our hated rival—Churchill High—was playing against our lesser-hated rival—Whitman High—on Saturday afternoon. This was a huge local game as Churchill was undefeated at that point and was marching toward the state playoffs.

From a football standpoint, we thoroughly despised Churchill. It was the lowest form of athletic enmity—the kind that arises from the subconscious recognition that we simply didn't have the talent, speed or size to beat them. However, if we couldn't beat them on the field, maybe we could embarrass them in some other small and pointless way. Fueled by one too many cans of Strohs or Schlitz or Milwaukee's Best or whatever cheap, crappy beer we were drinking, the idea was hatched to head over to the Churchill football field and partake in a "Rambo" mission. In our vernacular, "Rambo" missions were inspired by the *Rambo* movie series starring Sly Stallone and involved late-night stealth adventures steeped in teenage delusions of grandeur . . . and often harmless mischief and gray-area vandalism.

The details are a bit fuzzy about who was sober enough to drive, and it could even have been me. At the time, I drove a big Chevy station wagon that drew its inspiration from the "Family Truckster" that amiably starred in the classic Chevy Chase movie *National Lampoon's Vacation*. It was big and blue and ugly, but it could fit eight guys and was often the vehicle of choice for transporting a gaggle of idiots to points both known and unknown.

We parked about half a mile from the Churchill football field, donned dark clothing and snuck up under the proverbial cover of darkness. We climbed over the exterior fence, crept along the back of the empty bleachers and approached the storage shed in the back corner of the grounds. With our collective paranoid and inebriated minds racing, we were prepared any second for a flash of spotlights or a piercing alarm, but everything remained dark and quiet.

Arriving at the door to the shed, we were giddily surprised to find the storage door unlocked. Silly Churchill groundskeepers, storage sheds ARE NOT for kids! Among all of the equipment and supplies inside the shed were three bags of white chalk used to line the football field. Exchanging only conspiratorial nods, we removed all three bags from the shed and carried them out to the 50-yard line. Now what? As we each looked from face-to-face, one of the guys simply shrugged and blurted out the word "penis." Nothing else needed to be said. It was perfect.

Barely containing our excitement and laughter, we proceeded to draw a giant chalk penis with super-sized testicles right smack in the middle of Churchill's sacred football field. It was a carefully crafted penis . . . one "laid" with a reverential attention to detail! In fact, I would daresay that we were all quite cocksure that this would go down as one of the better pranks in memory. Once our masterpiece was complete, we got the hell out of there.

Unfortunately, none of us went to the Churchill-Whitman game the next day, but we heard through the grapevine that despite the Churchill groundskeepers' best efforts to remove the image, the washed-out remnants of the giant chalk phallus were plainly obvious to all fans in attendance.

Opting for discretion over valor, we managed to keep this audacious exploit a secret until after we graduated, and we were never caught. It was truly one of the proudest moments of my adolescence and a story that has gotten tremendous traction at reunions and cocktail parties through the years! I guess I should have felt bad for plundering three bags of chalk. To ultimately atone, I plan to leave three bags of chalk to Churchill High School in my will!

CHAPTER FOUR

ABCs
and 123s

It's back-to-school time,
but where are our thinking caps?

Lunchtime Dancing

by
Phil Silver

In the 1960-61 school year, I was an eighth grader at David Star Jordan Junior High School in Burbank, California. It was a fine institution for its time and had everything a kid could want.

I was a track-and-field athlete, and the school had a very nice running track. I was never the top finisher in running events, because my friend Kenny always managed to beat me just at the finish line. However, nobody could beat my broad jumps, as they were called back then. Today, the sport is known as the long jump.

But that's not what this story is about. I was also a theater major. The school had a very nice auditorium/theater where everything from school assemblies to choir concerts to stage plays took place. I performed in every school production, but that's not what this story is about, either. No. This story is about a young 14-year-old eighth-grade boy coming of age—going through the gene pool, so to speak—along with every other kid in the class.

There was a girl in my class named Wendy. In seventh grade, she was very pretty, with shoulder-length, brownish-blond hair, green eyes, and was always nicely dressed, but nothing especially remarkable stood out to me. However, Mother Nature had done wonders for Wendy during the summer vacation leading into eighth grade. When she returned to school, she had breasts. I don't mean little mounds held firmly in place by a bra under a pink, mohair sweater. I mean big, beautiful, Dolly-Parton-sized breasts that put lust in the heart of every boy at school. Yes, Wendy was quite an eye full, and I had a crush on her.

School started promptly at 8 A.M., lunch at noon and dismissal at 3 P.M. Lunch breaks were always my favorite part of the school day and served as a reference point, like an island in the ocean or an oasis in the desert. They were a welcomed resting point for me in the middle of the day. And rainy-day lunches were the best.

On rainy days—when we couldn't go outside after eating—we would have lunchtime dances in the gym. The event always started the same way: the lunchtime proctor would play an ever-changing mix of rock 'n' roll and slow music on 45 rpm vinyl records, while the boys stood against one wall and the girls, the opposite. Both groups stared at each other from across the room, deciding who we each wanted to dance with.

On this one particular rainy day, the first song played had a fast tempo. I didn't like dancing fast because doing so made me sweat. I guess no one else liked it, either, because no one was dancing. I preferred slow dancing, and as luck would have it, the next song was a slow one—*Blue Velvet*. That was it. That's all I needed to make my move. But I needed to get to Wendy before the other guys. She was my goal, and when we entered the gym I had positioned myself for this exact moment by standing directly across from her.

As soon as the music started playing, I made my dash. I wasn't alone. Out of the corner of my eye I could see my arch nemesis from the track team, Kenny, heading directly toward Wendy. We glanced at each other, but my positioning gave me the edge I needed. For once, I beat Kenny to the finish line! He graciously backed off, and I walked up to Wendy and asked her to dance. She agreed and we stepped onto the floor with all the other couples.

It was a dream come true, dancing with Wendy and her newly-developed breasts. There we were—Wendy's head on my shoulder and my head against hers—with my wondering eyes straining to get a glimpse of her beautiful lobes. Pressing ever closer brought to mind a quip I had heard Red Skelton make at the end of one of his television shows—a thank you to a very well-endowed Gina Lollobrigida, who was a guest on his show. After he hugged her and stepped back, he said, "Geez, I think I broke 'em both." Then he deadpanned the camera and said in typical Skelton fashion, "Aw, come on, folks. I meant my cigars," producing two broken cigars from his breast pocket.

It was only then that it dawned on me that "breaking 'em" was the least of my worries. The dance was ending, and suddenly I realized I had a problem: Jerry Seinfeld's definition of shrinkage was happening to me in reverse—BIG TIME. Fortunately for me, the next song was an up-tempo surfer song.

I quickly glided Wendy to the sidelines, and before everyone else had cleared the floor or noticed my bulging blue jeans, I began dancing again, this time by myself. Thank God *shrinkage* started to take effect.

I also danced the next dance alone, hoping my nether-region would fully retreat. I was also concerned that if I danced with Wendy again, my boner would return. There was a new dance step out—the Surfer Stomp—and I did my best to do it justice and still look cool in the process. Thinking back, it probably looked more like a cross between an Indian rain dance and someone walking across a bed of hot coals. I stomped all over that gym floor, swirling and twirling. I could hear my friends cheering me on, so I kept dancing until the song ended. Thankfully, the bell rang, signaling the end of lunch. As we all headed out the gym doors, my friends came up to me and said, in language of the day: "That was boss," "Bitchin' man, bitchin'," and "That was really cool."

The next day it was still raining, and all through my morning classes I dreamed of dancing with Wendy again. But when lunchtime came and I headed to the cafeteria, I passed the gym where I saw a sign posted on the door: "No dancing today. Gym floor being resurfaced."

My lunches were always a surprise because I never knew what my mom had packed. Usually it was a chipped beef or meatloaf sandwich, but one day it was a spaghetti sandwich. If it fit between two slices of bread, it was lunch, regardless of how strange the combinations were. Fortunately, today it was tuna fish.

While eating lunch and bemoaning the fact that I wouldn't

get to dance with Wendy, Kenny came up to me and said the gym floor was being resurfaced because it had a lot of scratches and pin holes in it. He said no more and walked away.

I didn't give Kenny's strange comment a second thought until much later that day. When I got home from school that rainy afternoon, I kicked off my wet, high-top, black Keds and reached for my more comfortable and dry huarache sandals. You know, the ones with the rubber-tire soles. But when reaching for them, I got a surprise—I pricked my finger on a tip of a nail sticking though the soles of one of the sandals. Taking a closer look, I noticed that numerous nail tips were poking through the rubber soles on both sandals.

It was then I put two and two together and realized what Kenny was trying to tell me: I was the last one on the gym floor and I was wearing these very same huarache sandals! I was the one who destroyed the gym floor!

Being careful not to stick myself again, I grabbed the sandals and quickly ran out to the garage, got a big hammer from my dad's tool chest, and destroyed the smoking-gun evidence by pounding the nail tips flat. I never wore my rubber-tire-soled huaraches to school again.

To this day, Wendy and I are still very good friends. However, I don't think she ever realized I had a crush on her back in the eighth grade. As for her knowing about my spontaneous and brief dip in the gene pool during our slow dance, I'll never know. And the gym floor, as far as I know, has been fine ever since it was resurfaced all those many years ago when I nailed it and lost out on another chance to do some rainy day dancing with Wendy.

The "B" Word

by
Anola Pickett

In 1946, I was in the fifth grade in a Kansas City, Missouri, parochial school. I'd never much minded always being the tallest person in my class until that spring, when I became aware of boys. They were no longer just loud, messy creatures like my brothers. For reasons I wasn't yet clear about, boys suddenly became worthy of my attention, and I wanted to be worthy of theirs. Besides being tall, I was also smart and read a lot and knew how to look up things in the dictionary—a talent that was to earn me male attention—and also to get me in a lot of trouble.

The only boys who came close to matching my height were the four who were older because of having flunked a grade or two. This male quartet and I sat together at the back of the room. The boys were there because they were literally in the room's backseat of learning. I was there because no one could see the blackboard if I sat up front.

Although we had little in common other than our shared space, we had an unspoken, loosely defined respect for one another. I never called them "dummies," the class label for the group, and they never called me "Grandma," the nickname given to me by some playground bullies. Serenely keeping company with the five of us, a plaster statue of the Virgin Mary smiled down from her corner pedestal, bestowing a saintly dignity to those of us assigned to last place.

One muggy afternoon, typical of a Kansas City spring, the sweet scent of peonies and spirea hung in the heavy air around the May altar set up in front of Mary's statue. We were writing our weekly spelling words the prescribed 10 times each when the boy to my right got my attention.

"Pssst! Anola!"

I turned to see him grinning at me. His pimpled face gleamed in the late afternoon heat. Pimples were a status symbol in fifth grade. Most of us hadn't sprouted so much as a blackhead.

Too timid to risk being caught "psssting," I raised my eyebrows.

He understood my signal. "Will you look this up for us?" He held a sliver of tablet paper on which a word was scribbled in pencil.

I nodded vigorously, delighted to be asked to help, and reached for my Webster's.

My neighbor grinned again and passed me the word.

I looked at it and opened to the B section.

The back-of-the-room boys were impatient. Their whispered "Hurry!" and "Found it, yet?" spurred me on.

I hunted through the B pages frantically. I had to find that word for the boys! If I failed them, they might never ask me to do anything for them again. They'd probably never speak to me again, much less smile or call out, "Pssst! Anola!" and pass me a note. Other girls would continue to get their notes, but this could be my one and only.

Search as I might, that B word simply was not in my *Webster's School Dictionary*. It was probably spelled wrong—none of my back-row-boys got more than 40 percent on any of our weekly spelling tests.

I turned around and whispered, "Are you sure this is how it's spelled?" Waiting for a reply, I failed to notice the swift passage of Sister Mary Theodosia down the aisle. I didn't hear the soft click of the huge black rosary beads that swung from her belt as she sailed toward my desk.

The four boys snapped up, straight and still at their desks. With one smooth motion, Sister snatched my dictionary and slammed her pointer on my desk with such force that the B word bounced up and fluttered—unnoticed—to the floor.

I went home that day commissioned to write a punishment sentence 500 times: "I will not talk during spelling class." Before going to my room to complete this task, I sought out an authority I trusted even more than Noah Webster. I was sure my mother could provide me with the information needed by my four backseat buddies.

She was taking down wash in the side yard. Wasting no time, I asked her about the word while we folded a sheet together.

"Mama, what's a 'bastard?'"

In the next few minutes my mother taught me three things:

1. The B word is not spelled with a double S nor an E.

2. It means someone "born out of wedlock."

3. A smart girl doesn't do something just because a boy asks her to.

Anola

Anola and her dad

First Chair

by
Elsilee Patterson

Looking at the postcard about my upcoming 50th high school reunion brought back the memory of "First Chair" and my sophomore year. I don't remember exactly how the coveted First Chair prize started in Mr. Loptien's science class—it was just one of those serendipitous happenings he let evolve, a way to encourage his students to do better.

Mr. Loptien's classroom was neatly arranged in five rows of six desks each, and at the beginning, nothing in the desk arrangement distinguished a First Chair from any of the others. But when several class members proposed that whoever got the highest score on almost anything graded would have the honor of sitting in First Chair, everyone else in class agreed. It was decided that First Chair would be the first desk in the first row.

For me, taking the title of First Chair was right up there with earning honor roll grades, something I did all the time.

The prize was not only motivation to continue doing well academically, but more importantly, I perceived it as an opportunity to gain respect from my peers over my nerdy penchant for getting high grades.

Earning First Chair was a snap, but the recognition I had hoped for wasn't! I pretended to my classmates that their collective efforts to dethrone me didn't bother me all that much—the harder they tried, the harder I studied and the more determined I became to stay there. With midterm approaching, I studied every spare moment I could until I knew any material possibly appearing on that exam backward, forward, upside down and inside out.

On the day of the midterm, while smugly ensconced in First Chair, I perceived my confident smile matched by one from Mr. Loptien as he placed the test in front of me. I was convinced beyond any doubt that I had this in my pocket! Glancing at the first page I thought, *Huh?* Rapidly flipping through the rest of the pages, I realized in horror I couldn't remember a single thing! My mind started racing, moving rapidly from, *Oh, my God, I'm going to lose First Chair!* to *Whoa! What if I flunk the midterm?*

I was so upset that I didn't notice Mr. Loptien standing beside my desk until he whispered, "Elsilee, what's wrong? Your face is turning blue!"

"Mr. Loptien," I sniffed quietly, "I've studied so hard for this but my mind is a total blank!"

Speaking softly, but loud enough for my classmates to hear, he said, "What you have is a mental block that we should be able to break by my asking you a simple question or two, so you can go on with the test. Now, how many feet are there in a yard?"

Taking a moment to think, I tentatively answered, "Twelve?"

"That's close, but you just told me how many inches there are in a foot and the question was, 'How many feet are in a yard?'"

It seemed like forever before I realized I knew the answer. "Three!" I exclaimed with conviction.

"That's right," Mr. Loptien replied. "Now take the test."

I felt quite foolish about not being able to remember those simple measurements. However, I actually enjoyed participating in the good-natured ribbing I received from my classmates about how I was able to keep First Chair only because our teacher gave me "special help."

Later that week, when the bell rang, thus dismissing us from science class, I was surprised when some of my classmates came up and asked me if I would like to go to the student lounge with them. Eagerly getting up to join them, I wistfully glanced back at my now empty chair—First Chair. It was then I pleasantly realized that this new feeling of belonging to the group had become a far more important first!

The Donut Snitch

by
Ann Marie Brick

It wasn't easy being a chubby sixth grader in 1960, especially because there were so few of us. In my Catholic school class of 48, there were only two: Margaret and me.

As was the custom, all sixth-grade girls were expected to sing in the choir for the daily 8 A.M. Mass that preceded school. Back then, church rules mandated fasting (no food or drink) after midnight right before receiving Communion—which we were all expected to receive—and that was a challenge for me. This ritual occurred about halfway through the morning service. "Going to Communion," as it was called, consisted of filing down the creaky, wooden, spiral staircase from the choir loft to the altar. The choir loft was situated above the back pews of the century-old church. The altar was in the front of the church. The 22 or so choir girls were expected to get downstairs—quickly and quietly—to the altar, receive the body and blood of Christ, and return to singing in approximately 10 minutes.

I could hardly wait till after Mass was over, because then we got to eat our breakfast. Mine consisted of a cup of Special K and a half pint of skim milk. I assume my mother prepared this for me because of the "chubby issue," but I longed to have chocolate Long Johns and powdered sugar donuts like my nemeses, Paulette, and her best friend, Cathy. They were perfect. The boys all wanted them to be their girlfriends. They were held up by the nuns and parish priest for the rest of us feckless preteens as role models of comportment. Oh, and did I mention they were tall and slender, as well? It was too much.

We all walked to school back then. I lived a block away— they lived three blocks away and passed the bakery on their morning trek to Mass. During the 10 minutes of the Communion ritual, the paper bags labeled with our names and containing our respective breakfasts were stored with our books in the back of the choir loft. Because of the age and condition of the old church, there had been a couple of instances of mice invasions into the breakfast sacks. That gave me an idea. I knew I could count on Margaret to join me. We would execute a faux mouse invasion on Paulette and Cathy's breakfast the next morning.

Our plan went like clockwork. Rushing downstairs to Communion, we returned to the choir loft before the others. I took Cathy's sack, Margaret took Paulette's. We punctured a finger-sized hole in each bakery bag, and then took a giant bite out of each of their pastries. Ha! They would discover the desecration when we got to class, and then they'd squeal and toss their breakfasts!

Unfortunately, that's not how it went. When Margaret and I got to the classroom, Paulette and Cathy were conferring with the nun. As we entered, they both pointed at me. In my haste to execute the perfect crime, I hadn't noticed the copious amount of powdered sugar displayed down the front of my navy blue uniform. Wow! Talk about rushing to judgment! Margaret wasn't even implicated and did nothing to confess her role in the donut debacle. I was summoned to the office. The gist of the reprimand was, "Not only did you steal and defile your classmates' breakfasts, you did it while the body and blood of Christ were still in your stomach!"

Before the imposition of my one-day suspension, I was sent to report my misdeed to the nearly deaf choir teacher, Sister Alphonsus, who looked about 80. She left her classroom to meet me in the school hallway. The doors to the other classes, grades one through eight, were all open. I tried to be discreet. "Sister, I have to leave choir because I took a bite out of Cathy and Paulette's donuts after Communion." I wasn't going to add the sin of ratting out my partner-in-crime.

"Whaaat did you say? Speak louder!"

God, I needed a megaphone for this woman. I had to repeat my transgressions several times—each time louder than the last. I was certain the whole school knew I was going to hell.

My mother arrived to take me home, where I had a lot of time to reflect on my actions. She was truly perplexed and kept asking—rhetorically, I think—"What were you thinking?" Obviously, I wasn't preoccupied with cause and effect.

That's why when I returned to school, I just knew that

those two would have to pay. I had to miss recess for a week and instead copy the Baltimore Catechism 2: "Why did God make you? God made me to show his goodness and to make me happy with Him in heaven."

Well, it seemed to me that God favored skinny girls. They had seats in front of the sixth-grade nun who bestowed every perk on those who were clearly the "teacher's pets." I sat in the back of the room next to a bulletin board. The board was filled with straight pins that secured colored construction letters that spelled out sappy sayings exhorting us to better behavior. I was focused on the straight pins.

After the class settled in from recess and before the nun could dispatch Paulette or Cathy on one of her pet errands, I made my move. Pulling two of the straight pins from the board, I walked up behind the two snitches and punctured their behinds. Their screams startled the nun right off her chair.

As my mother led me home for my second suspension voicing her exasperated phrase "What were you thinking?," I told her simply, "As they say in prison, 'snitches get stitches.'"

Where I had heard that, I can't recall, but I do remember thinking that perhaps I had been paying attention to the wrong sayings.

Spelling Bee Blues

by
Annmarie B. Tait

As a kid, the words "spelling bee" churned a considerable amount of acid in my stomach. In fact, my history of spelling bee fiascoes grew so notorious that Daniel Webster turned in his grave every time I stood up and headed for the contestant line.

Most of the time, striking me out of the competition didn't take long at all. I rarely made it past the second round. Yet with all that free time, it never occurred to me even once to bone up for the next match. Watching others spell words with ease, confidence and, above all else, correctness, consumed me. Worse than that, my teacher, Miss Divine, had a dome-shaped bell on her desk that she slapped with the palm of her hand to ring out the triumph of every classmate who spelled a word perfectly. The clang of that thing pierced my heart straight through. Oh, how I ached for the skill necessary to hear that bell dinging for me!

One classic spelling bee disaster occurred in the sixth grade and involved a word most fourth graders could breeze through—"cheese." I simply refused to believe that any one-syllable word could contain three E's that were practically right next to each other. How absurd! So there I stood, visualizing the challenge word, knees knocking and fingers nervously twirling through the curls in my pigtails.

"Cheese," I said, stepping forward. "C-h-e-a . . ."

I figured the ripple of snickers spreading through the class meant things weren't going so well. Still, I forged ahead like an Olympic figure skater skidding across the ice, flat on my face and heading straight for the judges.

" . . . s-e, cheese," I finished.

"I'm sorry. That's not correct, Annmarie. Please sit down."

The thin veil of sympathy on Miss Divine's face did little to disguise her disgust. Let's face it—I wasn't attempting to spell "pneumonia" or "ratatouille." A sixth grader plummeting to defeat on a first-round word like "cheese" can fling a teacher—lickety-split—into the disgust zone. Miss Divine proved no exception to that rule.

I dragged myself back to my desk still smarting from the sting of Miss Divine's invitation to take a seat, and plunked down just in time to hear the class smarty-pants throw those three E's into the word in all the right places. He barely finished before that old bell was dinging again.

After the agonizing cheese incident, my phonetic confidence plunged to an all-time low. The mere mention of a spelling bee triggered gastrointestinal disturbances in my belly strong enough to measure on the Richter scale. Nevertheless, despite the mountains I imagined from tiny molehills, I survived the spelling bee blues. Sadly, though, my spelling skills never really improved much.

A few years ago I discovered my older sister Marie suffered a very similar spelling bee trauma in the very same classroom, with the very same teacher—just two years before it happened to me, which may have explained the disgusted look Miss Divine directed my way that day. "Business" was the word that stumped my sister. Or as she spelled it: "b-i-z-n-e-s-s." It was such a relief to know that I was not the only sibling in my family with faulty spelling chromosomes.

Every once in a while I fantasize about writing to Miss Divine and telling her that my sister and I own a fabulously successful "CHEASE BIZNESS." I can see it now. As she reads the letter, she faints dead away, and her head lands right on the old dome-shaped bell, at last setting off one resounding clang for the phonetically challenged.

First Grade Olive Branch

by
Joyce Rapier

We all had first-grade stomping grounds. Some were memorable and others were not.

As a small child, my senses took in every aspect of my school, right down to the color of the brick walls and the smell of chalk and crayons. During the 1950s, although my school wasn't all that large, it appeared massive. The northeast side of the L-shaped school building housed first-grade classes and progressed in age toward the northwest. As a child got older, the southwest devoured third and fourth grades, and then the south quad of the building grabbed the fifth- and sixth-grade students. With its crank-out windows, steamy radiators and massive thick walls, the school seemed determined to squelch unruly kids and enforce a staunch educational code.

I will never forget my first day of school. As Mother and I walked nine blocks to a building that would confine me for eight hours, my stomach flitted. She assured me everything would be fine and told me to behave. *Me? Behave?* I thought to myself. *Shoot, you're always telling me I'm too outspoken and sassy.*

My first-grade teacher was a cheery person and when we entered the classroom, she greeted us all with a wide smile. Directing us to our chairs, she grinned the entire time and soothed those who cried over having been torn from their mothers' apron strings. She wore the sweetest fragrance, one that reminded me of daffodils. Neatly attired, with her brown hair coiffed in a bun, our teacher guided all of us with authority. I adored her instantly.

My desk was in the center of the room, right next to that of a curly-haired girl, whose temperament was as fiery as her red hair. We took one look at each other and knew blistering hell was going to break loose. While putting away our pencils, crayons and wide-margined writing paper, this girl dropped her crayons to the floor. I reached over to help pick them up when, without warning, my right arm and hand were suddenly void of skin. *Holy Minerva!* Her catlike claws, sharper than razor blades, uncoiled from the tips of her fingers and ripped the daylights out of me. The fight was on and 25 kids screamed bloody murder when I grabbed her by the hair and pushed her forehead into the desk, all the while she continued extracting blood from my arm. We were raging battle akin to Patton's push. The teacher separated us, but she knew this battle wasn't over.

Jungle gyms are always magnets for kids. During our first recess, we gravitated to the one on our playground like bees to honey. Since it was the first day of school, everyone wanted a chance to climb to the top bar, but that was impossible to do since there were so many of us. Diplomatically, we all decided to take turns in order of the first letter of our given name.

When it was my turn, I began to scale the octagon-shaped rungs, but my ascent was short-lived. My nemesis grabbed me by my foot and jerked me down to the ground, telling me it was her turn. Pulling out some of my baby-fine, white pony-tail, she shoved it into her pocket. I was mad, downright mad. One way or another, I was going to cure her of slashing me with her claws and pulling out my hair. *The heck with what Mother said—I'm going to show her!*

After recess, we marched back into class. All sweaty, I sat at my desk, she at hers. Out of the corner of my eye, I recognized the bright-red fingernail polish on my adversary's finger-tips slowly inching their way in my direction. She was in full fight mode and come hell or high water, she would soon find out I was no pushover.

Her hand was now in close proximity and I was deter-mined to engage my defense mechanism. Furtively, I bent over, took off one of my heavy-saddle, oxford shoes and slammed it as hard as I could on her hand. My shoe and her fingernails made contact. BAM! She cut loose with a few choice words, spewed very loudly, I might add. No, my swat didn't break her fingers, but it did snap several fingernails into shards.

Our teacher, knowing full well what had just happened, didn't say a word. Instead, she made her way over to our desks and told me to put my shoe back on. Reaching into her pocket, she then took out a fingernail clipper and proceeded to cut off all of my enemy's fingernails, which she gave to me. *Yuck!*

The next day, much to our teacher's chagrin, she was waiting for both of us before school, planning to tell us girls that if we provoked each other or instigated another battle, she would have to take us both to the principal's office.

But we had a secret—unbeknownst to our teacher, the Claw Queen and I came face-to-face after school that very first day. During that meeting, we stared at one another for what seemed to be an hour, antagonizing the other to advance first. With no luck drawing the other out, our meeting became a stalemate, an unusual and quiet repose. Then we started to laugh over our predicament. There we stood, she, with a clod-hopper-whopped, goose-egged forehead and swollen fingers, and me, with an abyss of gouged skin and no hair. We looked like two idiots wondering what to do next.

It didn't take too long to work toward a truce. On the school grounds, we knelt together in the corner of the L-shaped building. Using a small twig, we dug a hole and she gave me back my hair and I gave her back her fingernail clippings. Together, we buried everything.

It was our olive branch.

Fevers

by
Terri Elders

Sneezing and sniffling, I pressed a palm to my forehead. No fever, but I still wondered if I could convince Mama that I should skip school. I'd sip chicken soup and listen to daytime radio soaps with her. That sounded like a lot more fun that Miss Warren's geography quiz.

Today's quiz would be particularly tough. We had been studying bodies of water. I was all right so long as we stayed on land. I knew that Montpelier, Vermont was the nation's smallest capital, and Pierre, South Dakota was the second, and that they didn't rhyme, even though they looked like they should.

I knew all the countries and their capitals in South and Central America, and most of those of Africa, so long as they stayed put and didn't change their names. But there was something about the world's bodies of water that stymied me.

I could rattle off the names of the oceans and point to them on the classroom globe. But the North Atlantic Drift, the Antarctic Circumpolar Current, the Indian Ocean Gyre—these seemed more like chants to me and they didn't even stay in one place. The words had a nice poetic rhythm, but since I couldn't find them on the map, I wasn't even sure they existed.

When Miss Warren claimed we all had to become sea savvy to pass seventh-grade geography, I whispered to Stephen, who sat to my left, that I could hardly wait until we moved on to history.

"I'll never get sea fever," I confessed. "Bodies of water just confuse me."

What was the difference between the Gulf Stream and the Gulf of Mexico? So far as I could tell, one flowed out of the other, but which one did what baffled me. And why they were both in the Atlantic Ocean simply didn't make sense. When my family visited the Baja California coast of Mexico, we camped along the Pacific. When I squinted out across the waves, I tried to spy the coast of China, not Spain!

Mama came into the bedroom and peered down my throat. *Peer is how they pronounce that South Dakota capital,* I reminded myself, *not like that Pierre who got eaten by a lion in my favorite Maurice Sendak book.* "It's only one syllable," Miss Warren reassured the class as we exchanged puzzled glances. Not a one of us really believed that, but she seemed so sincere that we nodded solemnly and repeated it after her. *Peer—Peer, South Dakota.* "It's not *pee*-air," Stephen had whispered, giggling softly as he emphasized the first syllable.

"I think you just have hay fever," Mama said, going to my closet and pulling out a blouse. "It's spring and the air is full of pollen."

Right before class, I ran into Stephen, and we talked about the previous night's game. We had Dodger fever and agreed how this might finally be the year we won the pennant.

Miss Warren told us there would be 10 questions on the quiz. She would read the clues one at a time and give us a minute or two to write our answers. "Remember to keep your answers covered. This is the honor system, and I want to help you all be honorable."

I took a deep breath and glanced at Stephen. He smiled reassuringly. He shared my confusion about capes and channels and coves.

At first I thought I would be doing all right, scribbling my answers quickly. *Polar ice caps, English Channel, Angel Falls, Lake Superior.* Finally, there was just one more clue.

"Ponce de Leon discovered this in 1513, and then Spanish sailing ships used it when they sailed between Spain and the coast of Florida," Miss Warren said.

Oh, no, I thought, *It's one of those Gulfs, but which? Gulf Stream? Gulf of Mexico?* I gnawed on my pencil then took a chance. *Gulf of Mexico,* I wrote. I looked up. Stephen had his eyes fixed on my paper. I stifled a gasp as he wrote something on his own sheet. I was certain he had copied my answer before I could slap my hand over it. And my answer might be wrong.

We started our reading assignment while Miss Warren corrected our papers. I began to forget about Stephen as I lost myself in the fascinating new chapter about atolls and archipelagoes. They might be in water, but they didn't move around.

Suddenly I heard my name called. And Stephen's. "I want the two of you to come with me," Miss Warren said, opening the door into the hallway.

When we got outside she shifted her gaze from one face to another, back and forth like a pendulum. "Well? Who copied whom?" Miss Warren looked disappointed, but she kept her voice low. "You were the only two in the room who wrote *Gulf of Mexico* when it should have been *Gulf Stream*, and I don't think it's a coincidence that you sit next to one another."

We were dead in the water. I began to consider the possibilities. If I told the truth, that I saw him copying me, our budding friendship would be at an end. And Stephen was the only boy in seventh grade who shared my loyalty to the Dodgers, the only boy I could talk to without stuttering and stammering. Plus he had such a cute smile.

If I lied and said I had copied him, I'd get an unsatisfactory in conduct, and my parents would ground me forever. I made a silent vow that if he confessed, I would name my first-born son after him. Or, if it were a girl, it could be Stephanie.

The silence lengthened as I pictured my future twins, Stephen and Stephanie. Just as I started to ponder what I could name the third if they turned out to be triplets, Miss Warren again spoke, but this time not quite so softly. "Well?"

Finally, I opened my mouth. "I made a mistake," I began, but Stephen jumped in before I could complete my sentence.

"I'll take the blame," he blurted out. "I copied her. I didn't have time to review last night, and I forgot about Ponce de Leon."

Miss Warren turned to me. "You didn't cover your answers?"

I started to cry. "I forgot to cover my answers," I confessed. Stephen dug in his pocket and handed me a tissue.

Miss Warren gave us each a stern reminder about how she did not tolerate cheating. "Since this is the first time this semester, I'll forgive you this once. But I never want this to happen again." I tucked the tissue into my pocket and sneaked a peek at Stephen. He looked very serious as he promised never to copy my work or anybody else's again. I forgave him on the spot for getting us both into trouble.

I did pass geography in spring of 1949. And that fall the Dodgers won the pennant. A woman of my word, nearly a decade later, I named my firstborn Stephen.

I understand now that the Gulf of Mexico is a sea, while the Gulf Stream is indeed a stream. But, forgive me, it still seems slightly fishy to me.

Our Chinese Pagan Baby

by
Gregory Lamping

"Feed the piggy!" Sister Corrine kept telling us, all winter long. Come that spring, the pig was full. Our seventh-grade class had finally filled the pink, plastic piggy bank with our nickels and dimes and occasional quarters. On the side of the pig, written with a black magic marker, were the words PAGAN BABY.

As I understood it, our money was going to be sent to a Catholic missionary priest in China, home of the "Godless Pagans." He would supposedly go up to some Chinese mother holding her newborn and ask if he could baptize her baby by sprinkling Holy Water onto its forehead. "This will only take a few seconds, I promise," he would say, and if she balked, he would flash her a $5 bill, an offer she couldn't refuse.

Since it was our money, we were granted the privilege of naming the pagan baby. If the baby was a girl, the girls in our class would get to name her, but if it was a boy, we boys would name him.

It was time to decide on names. Sister Corrine instructed us to move our desks together into two groups—boys and girls. She then announced she was leaving and would return shortly to hear the names we had chosen.

With Sister Corrine now gone, none of us boys were too eager to say anything. We had been down this road before, ever since the fourth grade. Finally, a boy whom I'll call "Leonard Brownnose" suggested a name. Since his First Holy Communion, and in his polite *Leave it to Beaver* Eddie Haskell voice, Leonard had been telling the nuns that he was going to someday become a priest, maybe even the Pope. But to us, he was a snitch. The nuns loved him; we hated him.

"I say we name him Joseph," he said, "after Saint Joseph, the father of Jesus. That's also the name of our pastor, Father Joseph Little."

We all looked down in silence before one of the guys, a boy who had been snitched on many a time, said, "Screw that name! I say we call him Porky Pig." I imagine he had glanced over at the piggy bank for his inspiration.

"Let's name him Bugs Bunny!" another boy said. We seemed to be going *Looney Tunes*.

"No, we should name him Elmer Fudd," said another boy. "Elmer Fudd is a human; Bugs Bunny is a rabbit."

"What about calling him Stinky!" yet another boy chimed in.

The Chinese woman who took our money wasn't going to give a hoot what we named him, since she was probably going to keep whatever name she had originally given her kid and just pocket the loot. But that didn't dampen our imaginations.

I began thinking. I thought of the titles and authors of these books I had come across in *Sick*, a magazine for degenerate schoolchildren, such as *Rusty Bedsprings* by I. P. Knightly and *Fifty Yards to the Outhouse* by Willy Make It. My favorite was *Brown Splotches on the Ceiling* by Hoo Flung Poo.

Hmm, I thought to myself. *Hoo Flung Poo!*

"Hey, I got an idea," I said to the group. "Since we're naming a Chinese baby, why don't we give him a Chinese name? Why not name him . . . " I shared the name quietly, so the girls wouldn't hear me. The boys howled, especially once I mentioned the title of the book this author had written. They said it was a great name, and that I should be given the honors of telling Sister Corrine the name we had chosen, since, after all, it was my suggestion. I agreed, since we were having such fun.

Sister Corrine stepped back into the classroom. She looked somber, as if she were a judge awaiting our verdict.

"Well, girls, did you come up with a name for your pagan baby?"

This girl, who I'll call "Miss Straight A's" stood up and said, "Yes, we have."

"Well?"

"Christina Angela Marie."

All of us boys were thinking the same thing, *Good God, how much more Catholic could you get? Jesus Christ, the Blessed Virgin Mary and all the angels in heaven packed into one precious name.*

"And you boys," she said, now directing her attention to us. "Did you decide on a name?"

It got so quiet, I could hear myself sweat.

"Yeah, I guess so," I said, slowly rising from my desk.

Sister Corrine stared me in the face with her piercing blue eyes. My group looked over at me with great anticipation, waiting to hear me utter the name we had chosen.

"It's ... uh ... Joseph!"

I listened for their reaction. I didn't hear anything from the guys, but could sense what they were thinking: YOU CHICKENED OUT!

"OK, class," said Sister Corrine, ready to move on. "Take out your readers and turn to page ... "

Gregory

Sibling Shenanigans

All in the Family takes on a
whole new meaning . . .

Up a Tree

by
Carole Fowkes

Evil sat across from me eating a tuna fish sandwich. I kept a wary eye on her as I drank my glass of milk. I never knew when my tormentor would strike, so I couldn't let my guard down.

When she finished her sandwich, she looked at me and grimaced. "How can you drink that stuff?" she asked. "Only babies drink milk." She sipped her Kool-Aid like it was a martini. "This is what grown-ups drink."

My mother, my savior, came into the kitchen. "Stop teasing your sister," Mom ordered. "Vicky, if you're done, go outside and play." My sister groaned and gave me a threatening "later" look as she sauntered out the door.

My sister Vicky was three years older than me, bigger and a whole lot meaner. Although she was kind to other kids and small animals, she nonetheless thrilled in bullying, teasing and otherwise making my life miserable. Like the time she'd convinced me to eat sauerkraut, which I loathed, telling me it was sweet kraut. Or when she ran me over with her bike because I didn't jump out of the way fast enough.

I took time to pull the crust off my sandwich and mashed it into a soft sphere. It was summer in Ohio and though a monstrous new trick devised by Vicky might await me, I couldn't resist the pull of the sun. That day it shone on me, and I struck a note for all younger siblings who'd been picked on, tormented or made to feel wretched. After my last sip of milk, I wiped my mouth and headed outside to play with Debbie, my latest best friend.

A few hours of intense playing with Debbie made me thirsty. I wanted some of that adult drink, Kool-Aid. Besides, Debbie wanted to play with her dolls, an activity I abhorred. A confirmed tomboy, I made it my mission to avoid playing with those plastic replicas of the real thing. Debbie, knowing this, wasn't too upset when I took my leave of her and her pudgy, curly-haired fake baby.

I ran inside my house and before anyone saw me, took a gulp of the sophisticated stuff, spilling more on the floor than I got down my throat. In our house, Kool-Aid was only for big kids. No matter! I wiped it up with my hand and dashed out before my mom caught me.

When I got outside, my enemy was waiting. "What're you doing?" Vicky asked.

"Nothing." I needed an escape, quick. "I'm gonna climb that tree over there." I pointed to a big maple in the field, almost hidden by weeds and bushes.

"You can't do that. Daddy says it's dangerous and he'll kill you if you do."

Ah! An opportunity to show up my big sister, I thought. I answered, "I don't care. I'm gonna climb it."

We raced to the forbidden tree, oblivious to the cuts and scrapes we received from the bushes. The tree was tall and half-way up, the trunk was split, so it looked like twin trees. I started to climb, but Vicky pulled me down by my shorts. "I want to do it. I'm faster than you and I'll be down before Daddy gets home."

My lower lip pushed out involuntarily. "You always get to do the fun things."

She climbed, huffing as she pulled herself up, finally resting in the spot where the trunk split. Her voice shook. "OK, I'm coming down." But she couldn't move. The V-shaped space was big enough to get in, but now her bubble butt was wedged in like a piece of cheese in a mouse trap. "I'm stuck. Go get Mom."

I spun around to go, but stopped myself. For all nine years of my life, I'd been my sister's victim. I smiled. "No."

"Please?"

"No!" I shouted. Guilty joy coursed through me. "No!" I repeated. The heady thrill of revenge made me jump up and down. "No!" I said again and again.

As I walked away, I could hear Vicky's tearful threat. "I'll murder you when I get down!" She would, too, but for now, I was safe. I skipped off to play my favorite board game, believing myself to be the cleverest girl, ever.

When my father got home an hour later, we gathered

around the dinner table. My mother asked, "Where's your sister? She's never late for dinner."

I put my napkin in front of my mouth to hide my snicker. "I don't know."

My mother stuck her head out the door and yelled, "Vicky, get in here this minute!" But, of course, Vicky didn't answer. My mother turned to my father. "I hope nothing's happened. We better go look for her."

My father pushed back his chair and threw me a look that could chill the sun. "You better not be hiding something."

I cringed. How could I keep silent under his dark, suspicious gaze? I bent my head down until my chin rested on my chest. "She's in the tree."

He leaned in toward me, and I could smell the cigarettes on his breath. "What? What tree?"

"In the field. The one you told us not to climb."

He stood up. "Show me."

I led him to my sister's green, leafy prison. By now Vicky was near hysteria. "Daddy! Help me!"

My father shouted to her. "I'll get you down, Pumpkin! I'll get my ladder!" As he turned toward the garage, he threw me a look I knew meant I wouldn't live to see the sun rise.

With coaxing and tugging, Daddy got Vicky out of the tree. My mother comforted her and she got an extra dish of ice cream after dinner. When my mother asked her why she'd climbed the tree, since Vicky didn't like heights, Vicky looked straight at me and I wondered what it felt like to be skinned alive. I needn't have worried. Vicky shrugged her shoulders, "I just thought I should get over being scared of being up high."

My dad, who was the bravest person I knew, hugged her. "It's good to get over your fears." He looked at Vicky then at me and scowled. "But don't ever do something like this again."

Vicky didn't say anything about me leaving her in the tree for over an hour, and my parents didn't punish me for not telling on Vicky for climbing up that tree. When we went to bed that night, my sister smirked and whispered, "You owe me."

But she never collected on that debt. From that day on, our relationship shifted. Slowly I became her friend, but not when she was with others her own age—that would be too uncool. And together we weathered our family's frequent moves, our tumultuous teen years, early adulthood and marriage. I believe she now knows that I'd never leave her hanging up in a tree again—and I know she'd never tell on me.

Acting Alone

by
Anna Roberts Wells

The new pastor in my childhood town brought with him a love of movies. When he discovered that most members of his congregation could rarely make it to the theater in Little Rock, he found a movie distributor and set up Friday night movies in the church hall. Because they were being served up to good Christian people, the movies we saw were the classics— family fare, good westerns and war movies. We sat in folding chairs set up in rows with an aisle down the center. Some of the church ladies brought desserts and made lemonade, and there was plenty of time to enjoy fresh popcorn during breaks while setting up the next film on the one projector.

In that church hall, I fell in love with *Mutiny on the Bounty*, Fred Astaire and Ginger Rogers and Charles Laughton's Quasimodo from *The Hunchback of Notre Dame*. It was this last one that led to one of the less-than-stellar moments of my young life.

My grandmother, who lived with us, was a clothes horse and loved to shop. My father, perhaps out of appreciation for all she did for him and us, indulged her shopping by taking her to Little Rock on many Saturdays. As we got older, we were allowed to go with her, and by the time I was 11, she would let me take my sister for an hour or so to shop by ourselves at Woolworth's while she prowled the aisles of all the upscale department stores. The plan was always to meet at the side door of Pfeiffer's at the designated time. I had no idea that she ever went near any of the dime stores or the Rexall where we could get a soda and listen to the tableside jukeboxes. Because of this, I thought I was perfectly safe playing a little joke on the good shoppers of Little Rock.

We had just seen *The Hunchback of Notre Dame*, and I was taken with Laughton's performance. I talked my eight-year-old sister into leading me around our usual haunts while I pretended to be mentally and physically challenged. I took my posture and movements straight from Quasimodo. Jane had nothing to do but hold my right hand and coax me down the street as I limped and grunted along. I was getting quite a kick out of the pitying looks and comments, although one woman declared that people should keep such children out of the public eye. Her companion replied that at least I appeared to be clean and well cared for.

When I wanted to go to Rexall, I uttered a garbled sentence that sounded something like, "Woah gos geh ahh danck." Jane had no idea what I was saying, so I pretended to cry and pulled her in the direction of the drugstore. To my horror, and hers, our grandmother had had a yen for a Cherry Coke, a treat she sometimes allowed herself, and there she was coming out of Rexall as we were approaching. Jane saw her before I did because she dropped my hand abruptly and stepped away. It was a feeble attempt to distance herself from the titanic disaster she saw looming in my future. As I peered up from my hunched-over position, I caught the full blast of my grandmother's anger. She took one step forward and yanked me upright. Had the streets not been teeming with Saturday shoppers, I am not sure I would be here to tell this tale.

She did what she always did when she was about to lose her generally well-developed control—she spoke quietly through clenched teeth, a trait my children would say I inherited. I saw my life flash before me and was certain that the future held dire consequences if I could live long enough to see what they would be. She informed me that I was not to leave her side and we were going to march straight over to Allsopp and Chappel's Bookstore where my dad was a faithful and well-loved customer. When we got there, my father took one look at my grandmother—and her hand digging into my shoulder—and excused himself from his conversation with the owner.

We walked silently to the car, and silence reigned until we got home. My brother and sister peeked at me whenever they dared, but neither offered a sympathetic word of comfort. My grandmother and father conferred in the privacy of her bedroom before my father came out and told me that I was confined to my room for the week and would miss the next month of movies at the church. He seemed to be in total alliance with my grandmother, and I was ashamed that I had caused them so much grief. My brother and sister stayed as far away from me as they could for the rest of the day. Maybe they feared that some of my inherent evil would rub off on them.

Just when I thought I would be forever a disgrace to my family, my dad came in to say goodnight. As he leaned over to plant the customary kiss on my forehead, he murmured, "I would have loved to have caught your acting debut, but you'll have to live with your grandmother's decision." Just before he turned out the light, he gave me a big grin and a wink.

The
Three Musketeers

by
Randy Svisdahl

It was 1961. I was 10 years old and living on a farm in re-
mote Bella Coola, British Columbia, at the end of a mountain
road that led to nowhere.

Bella Coola is hidden on a section of Canada's northwest
coast, sheltered at tide line and surrounded by magnificent
towering mountains. It was a wonderful place for young boys
to grow up, and I was lucky to have brothers in such an isolat-
ed community. Since there were no televisions or video games
around back then to distract us or interest us, we all hung out
together.

At 17 years old, Gary was the oldest brother. One day, he
decided to take me and our 12-year-old brother Wylie on an
exploration trip up a side valley known as Nutsatsum. The goal
was to reach the head waters of the Nutsatsum River.

Because of the large grizzly bear population in the valley, our
mother was a bit hesitant and worried when Gary suggested the

trip. But he managed to talk Mother into letting us go, especially when he promised to pack in Dad's 1894 Winchester rifle just in case we had a run-in with a bear.

Being the youngest of the three, I was very excited about the trip. It was the beginning of a lifetime of incredible hiking in the mountains and forests of British Columbia. Even though it might not have been the smartest thing to do, we were three guys looking for adventure. And whenever I look back on that trip, I grin from ear to ear.

Our gear was easy to organize. First and foremost, we had an ax. Every boy in the valley had one. An ax was a right of manhood because of the wood that had to be cut for the winter. We also packed a knife and some rope and string for our adventuring, because we didn't know what we might run into or what dilemma we might find ourselves in. We packed bread, cheese, a little sausage and some fish in a jar. And Wylie—who loved spices—threw in salt and pepper. For sleeping, we decided a gray Army surplus blanket for each of us would do.

For backpacks, we used burlap potato sacks with a small rock in each bottom corner, tying the rocks with string to keep the packs flat and make them look like real backpacks. Then we tied off the top of the sacks with a half-inch-thick rope that we also used for straps. The plan was to fill the sacks with our supplies and tie the neck off, and then put our arms through the ropes and hoist them comfortably onto our backs.

We had no tent, but knew when we found a place to camp each night, we could construct a low shelter over where we planned to build a fire. And by adding moss to the fire to make smoke—which, of course, would bellow back into the shelter—the majority of mosquitoes that constantly plagued us during those warm summer days would keep their distance.

Once we three boys were geared up, we said our goodbyes and set off.

The habitat in the Nutsatsum Valley was old-growth forest with thick huckleberry and blueberry bushes. There was also a lot of devil's club—thick, snarly thorny shrubs that could tangle you up for hours if you were unlucky enough to get into them. The only trails to walk were wild, unpleasant and natural. Natsatsum Valley was jungle-like in its vegetation because it was rainforest, and the government had no groomed trails where we were heading. There were, however, bear trails everywhere, trails that meandered beside fast-flowing rivers where bears were often seen fishing.

Two days into our trip, we got onto higher ground and the view started to open up before us. We were excited about trying to find the headwaters, so we decided that in order to get there, we would need an extra day. That meant rationing our food. Unfortunately, because we were kids, we didn't know how to plan our meals like Mother would have done if we had told her how many days we'd be gone. Rationing our food added excitement to the adventure.

Later that day, as we were walking by one of the many rivers in that part of the country, Gary lost his footing and fell in. Having been the keeper of our supplies, the last of our rationed chow went down the river with him. Though Gary survived—soggy, grumpy and out of sorts—our food did not.

The loss of food suddenly became a huge dilemma. We were two days from the nearest road that would lead us back to civilization. But because we were having so much fun being real-life adventurers, we didn't want to leave. We took a vote. As there were three of us, the majority won. We were going to rough it and eat from the land.

That night, we huddled in front of a smoking fire, very hungry, not having fun but all pretending to. After all, what could we young boys do—admit we were not yet men? The next morning we started out again with nothing in our bellies, acting very brave and sacrificial. But, secretly, each one of us was sure he would, at any second, starve to death.

About midday, higher on the mountain, we came to a log on a major slough that had to be crossed. Wylie went first, easily balancing his weight on the narrow log. I followed, and Gary, carefully holding the Winchester, brought up the rear. But Gary got stuck on an offshoot log between two trees. He couldn't move, and he couldn't use the Winchester, which generally would not have been a problem.

But, that was when we saw the grizzly bear.

Three sets of wide eyes met the bear's narrow gaze and for a moment nothing moved—not a lash or a muscle or a cell. The air was charged with immobilizing fear. The bear snorted, grunted and pawed the ground. Suddenly, he charged. But it was a false charge. Turning, the grizzly vanished back into the woods, leaving us safe. Excitedly terrified, we hauled Gary out from his wedged position.

We safely crossed the log and came upon a half-consumed 30-pound salmon lying on the forest floor. We figured the grizzly had been eating it. The three of us stared at the salmon for some time, our stomachs grumbling. After some discussion as to what to do about the fish, we left it where it was, though we wanted to claim it for ourselves. But we were more scared the bear might get mad if we did, and worse, follow us to camp. We continued on our way, hungry and noble.

Later that afternoon, as we were crossing a small shallow creek with a sandy bar, I heard a splashing sound. I knew exactly what that meant! I leapt with glee toward the sound, and as luck would have it, with my bare hands I caught two cutthroat trout that had been trying to spawn. I must say it was the only time I could ever remember my two older brothers ever looking at me with such profound respect. As I held the silvery beauties in my triumphant hands, I could see awe on both of their faces. I reveled in that glory.

Shortly after we made camp, we wrapped our 4-pound cutthroat trout in foil liner we had the good sense to save from a box of instant mashed potatoes. We buried the fish under our campfire and let them cook, and then served the catch on devil's club leaves. Salt and pepper, which Wylie dug out of his potato sack, was added to taste, as were blueberries we picked on our way to the campsite.

That night, as we dove into our tasty meal—careful not to get fish bones stuck in our throats—a special memory was in the making, brewing sweet and smoky with sentiment for the future. Though I have taken many trips into the woods since that day, the adventure I took with my brothers the summer of 1961 was the most memorable. And it was also the most memorable childhood meal I have ever eaten.

We brothers survived a terrific adventure. We survived danger and hunger and fear. We three friends. Three brothers. Three musketeers.

Sibling Chivalry

by
Diana M. Amadeo

It was a particularly stressful day, and the kids were at it again. Lord knows I love them dearly, but the constant bickering, whining and tattling had become exasperating. They were young, but I worried this would carry on into their teens and maybe even adulthood. Would the sibling rivalry ever end? Would they ever become friends? I took these questions via telephone to my long-distance mother. Mom is an expert on sibling rivalry, having coped with it through 10 children.

"We never fought like that," I insisted to Mom.

A heavy pause came from the other end of the line. Then, finally, Mom asked, "What about you and Gene?"

Gulp. Got me on that one, I said to myself.

As kids, Gene and I probably gave Mom and Dad the most grief as we spoke our minds and demanded independence in a house with children everywhere. We were close in age and temperament. We both considered the religious life, and then thought again that being a nun or priest wouldn't work for us. We didn't take orders well.

It didn't take a genius to figure out that Gene saw me as a direct rival for Mom and Dad's attention. When I was a baby, he turned over my bassinet trying to steal my rattle. Over the years, try as I might, he never included me in his fun—especially when he was nine, and I was only eight years old.

It was bad enough that my brothers built a tree house and wouldn't let me help. But afterwards, Gene tacked up a sign that read, "Girls Not Allowed." What a creep. I tattled to Mom about his tree house. Usually Mom didn't pay much attention to tattling, so I was surprised when she yelled at him to come home.

"Gene, Diana tells me that you built a tree house at the end of the field."

"That's right," Gene said, just as proud as you please. "It's in the trees way over there." He pointed into the distance.

"Now, Gene," Mom began sternly, "that tree is too close to the railroad tracks. You could fall off a limb right onto the barbed wire fence. The county put that fence there to keep kids like you away from the tracks."

"Ah, Mom, I made a platform in it and everything. The guys love it. If you let us keep it, I promise that I'll make everyone clear out of it when a train goes by."

Mom was quiet for a minute. Surely she wouldn't fall for that line of gobbledygook. I couldn't believe it when she said, "OK, but keep on this side of the fence. No one goes near the tracks. And, oh, let Diana play in the tree house."

As it turned out, the tree house could have been great fun,

but Gene, my other brothers and his friends made life so miserable there that I didn't stay long. Besides, I had other things to do. That morning, Mom had promised that if I picked her a bucket of wild raspberries, I could make fresh raspberry sauce. There was nothing in the world like fresh, sweetened raspberries to scoop over a bowl of yummy vanilla ice cream.

So I ran back to the house and grabbed a bucket from the kitchen table. The wild raspberry bushes near the house were nice enough and the bees not so disturbing, so I picked there for a while. But these berries were small compared with the acres of raspberries in that forbidden territory—around the railroad tracks.

Making sure no one was watching, I dashed along the barbed wire fence until I found a spot where it sagged. Carefully, I stepped over the prickly fence and onto the gravel next to the tracks. There were lots of green bushes with their bright red raspberries—some as big as a penny, just ripe for the picking. I battled with the bees and began to fill my bucket.

The faint sounds of a train whistle blew in the distance. My heart began to race. *It's OK,* I told myself. *Just find the low spot in the fence and climb over.*

But I couldn't find the low spot. I raced back and forth along the fence. It seemed as though the sag had disappeared. The ground began to shake. The air was filled with the loud whine of the train's engine. Panicking, I stuck my head through the barbed wire and pulled my arms through. My shirt and pants were caught on the prickly thorns. I think I was screaming, but the train just drowned me out.

Then I felt someone's hand grab mine and give it a mighty tug. I didn't budge.

The train was inches away.

The hand that was pulling me let go. Quickly two arms appeared. They reached around my torso and hugged me. I buried my head into a bony shoulder, closed my eyes and cried. The train whizzed by so close I swear it brushed my backside.

Then all was quiet. I lifted up my head and wiped away my tears. I was so embarrassed. But my brother, Gene, looked even more embarrassed.

"Now look what you did! I'm bleeding!" he whined.

"I didn't make you hold me," I replied, worried how I would explain my own scratches.

"Fraidy cat, cry baby," Gene said.

"Squirrel bait!" I retaliated.

I carefully pulled myself and the bucket through the fence and raced home. We never talked about what happened. Surprisingly, Mom never asked about our wounds. But I think Mom figured out the act of chivalry when I gave Gene—my arch nemesis—an extra scoop of berry sauce on his ice cream that night.

Diana

One Prank Deserves Another

by
Susan Sundwall

I don't remember what I had going on that night, but when I got home, Mom informed me that my younger sister, Shari, had taken a babysitting job that was ordinarily mine. In a family of seven kids, money for extras was scarce and those sitting jobs were a nice little income stream for me. I babysat for about half of our immediate neighbors, as well as for others a few streets over.

Grumpy about missing out on the job, I headed for my room. Opening my dresser drawer, I took out an envelope— the one full of my babysitting money. Well, maybe not full, but the $7 inside represented a goodly number of hours, especially at 50 cents per hour. I hoarded every greenback in those days. But tonight, thanks to Shari, there wouldn't be any additional greenbacks to stash.

As the prankster in our family, I tucked my money away, and then thought of Shari watching the little girl and her brother only two doors down. As I stewed, the demon of pranking came and hopped onto my shoulder, and the brilliance of the plan he offered was too much to resist. *What if I put on that stupid vinyl coat Mom talked me into buying, the one that goes down to my ankles, and grabbed one of Dad's old hats from the hall closet, and go scare Shari?* It was a great plan! I would slither out of the house when no one was looking, sneak through the neighboring two yards to where Shari was babysitting, and surprise her! I knew the property there, both front and back. I knew the latch on their side gate had no lock. *Wouldn't it be hilarious to creep through the gate and knock on the back door, speak in a deep scary voice, and die laughing when Shari nearly passes out from fright?* My secret hope—and ultimate goal—was that she'd shriek and wet her pants.

I had to wait until everyone else in the house was busy before I could successfully launch my plan. My younger siblings were glued to the television, Mom was in her bedroom and Dad was in the garage. When it seemed safe, I grabbed the coat and hat and managed to get out of the house undetected. I quickly made my way across two lawns, hoping no nosy neighbors were outside at that hour. My heart was hammering as I put on the hat and coat. I got to the gate, slipped through and stood at the back door. I knocked.

At first nothing happened. The back door was off the laundry room and I could see light from the living room just beyond the washing machine. I figured Shari was in there on the sofa, watching television. The kids were probably already sound asleep. I knocked again—louder this time—and then saw her head pop around the corner into the dark laundry room.

"Who's there?" she asked, tentatively.

"Is Sharon here?" I replied, gruffly.

"What?" she said, still with only her head showing. Her eyes were huge!

"Is Sharon here?" I asked, a little louder.

"Who is it?" she asked in a shaky voice, gripping the wall. "What do you want?" Her terror was on the rise, and my mirth overflowed.

That's when I lost it. I whipped off Dad's hat and started laughing. "Did I scare you?" I gasped. I knew I had, but when she recognized my voice, she charged through the laundry room at me, shaking with rage. I got the prank gene and she got the rage gene—I should have remembered that!

"You creep!" she yelled, whipping on the back porch light. "You scared me to death. I didn't know who you were!"

Which was the point, I thought. But the wrath in her voice was palpable and what she said next wiped the joy off my face.

"I'm telling Mom! She's gonna kill you!"

Now, mind you, I'd sat at the sibling negotiating table many a time. This was the place where you brought your arsenal of held-back knowledge—knowledge of sister wrongdoings with which to negotiate. And now I had to bring out the big guns. Creeping around late at night in dark clothing and scaring the poop out of my younger sister was a mobster-worthy prank.

"If you do, I'll tell about you and Wendy smoking out behind the 7-Eleven," I shot back. Wendy was our next youngest sister.

"Oh, yeah? I saw you sneak out with that Roger guy the

other night! You were in the alley kissing him!"

Man, things were getting dicey here. *I'll have to be a bit more cautious with my sneaking out from now on.* We traded volleys for a while until I finally decided the only thing I could do was apologize. So I did. By that time, Shari had settled down, the kids had slept through our argument, and I skedaddled for home.

The next morning, Shari and I eyeballed each other across the breakfast table. Each knew what the other was thinking—to get even! And you probably already know this, especially if you've ever been accosted by the demon of pranking yourself: a good prank is something that just keeps on giving!

The Pest

by
Carol Brosowske

Life in the panhandle of Texas in the 1960s was much simpler than it is today. Sibling interactions, however, haven't changed much over the years. My older brother and I had a love-hate relationship that rivaled the best of them. We took turns tormenting each other. He was six years older and just getting into the girlfriend stage. One of my favorite things to do was to listen on the extension to his long, drawn-out phone conversations, especially when he was talking to a girl. Oh, the juicy conversations I overheard were a delight to me! But it was difficult to keep from laughing.

I never could keep my mouth shut. If I had, he never would have known I was listening. I could not help myself, teasing him and making kissing noises and reciting the rhyme, "Ed-die and Terri sitting in a tree, K-I-S-S-I-N-G. First comes love, then comes marriage, then comes Eddie with a baby carriage!" Oh how I loved taunting him with that little ditty and letting anyone else within earshot hear it, especially his friends. If he could have, he probably would have put me up for adoption back then, and there were many times when it was a good thing that I was a fast runner. I knew that if I ran to my mother, she would protect me. I knew he couldn't hit me in front of her. He would walk away, mad as heck, calling me a pest. He called me that all the time, and it never bothered me—until one certain day.

I was in the car with my mother, and we were running errands. I was sitting in the front seat feeling like I was something quite special, pretending I was a girl much older than my years. We stopped at a red light and a dark blue truck pulled up beside us. I started reading the words on the side of the truck. They read, "WE KILL PESTS!"

Oh no, could this be true? I thought. I was a pest—this I knew because my big brother had told me so. I had always known it. I got very nervous and my mouth went extremely dry. My head was spinning with horrid thoughts: *Snuffed out at the age of nine? I would never get to experience junior high school; I'd never get that Barbie outfit I was determined to buy with the money my grandmother had sent for my birthday. Nope, there was no turning back now. I was a goner.*

Surely I was reading that wrong, so I read it again and again to make sure. Yes, there it was in big black letters: WE KILL PESTS! I swallowed hard then turned to my mother, sniveling, "Oh, Mother, do they really?"

"Do they really what?" she asked, looking straight ahead, waiting for the signal to change.

"Kill pests," I said, pointing to the lettering on the truck.

She turned to view the big blue truck I was pointing to with my shaky little hand. She read it then answered, "Yes," very nonchalantly.

I knew it, I thought to myself, *it had been confirmed by the woman who knew everything, even the things you didn't want her to know. But how could she sit by so calmly?* I was in a terrible situation. Did I really deserve a death sentence simply because I was an irritating little sister? This woman I called "mother" seemed to have no feelings at all for my dilemma. I could not believe what I was seeing or what I was hearing; I thought she loved me, but how could I have been so wrong all these years of my short life? My suspicions had been confirmed—she really did like my brother best.

Finally the light changed, and we were moving again, but that truck was staying right there beside us. I looked at the man driving. He looked like a nice man. Was he going to do it right then? How was it going to happen? Was it going to hurt? And why wasn't my mother trying to turn or go faster and outrun that truck? We had a faster vehicle than he did. I knew we could do it if she just tried.

Frantic, I could be silent no longer.

"How can you let this happen?" I asked her, with tears streaming down my face.

"Let what happen?" she asked.

"That truck, it says they kill pests, and Eddie said I'm a pest!"

She started to smile, suddenly understanding my distress. "No, silly, they kill bugs, mice and critters that get in your house. All those things are called 'pests.' They're not going to kill you. They don't kill little girls!"

Oh, what a relief! I slumped back into the seat. It took a while before I stopped shaking and finally got my breathing back under control. It was such a good feeling when we got home at last, where I felt safe and secure once again.

I know my brother heard the story of that dark blue truck, and although he never mentioned it once, he continued to call me a pest—and he still does, 50 years later. I remain thankful to this day that I have not yet been exterminated—and I'm pretty sure that my big brother was finally able to enjoy some well-deserved laughter, at my expense.

Eddie (left) and
Carol

Farm Kids, Barns and Ropes

by

James Butler

I spent my first 10 years of life on a small quarter-section family dairy farm in Eaton County, Michigan with a sister two years younger. Being a kid on a farm is one great adventure after another, but things can get a bit out of hand when parents are not around.

One summer day I was watching a western on television when the hero tossed a rope over a tree and lowered himself into a ravine to escape the bad guys. That gave me a great idea. I had a rope. I had an empty upper-level feed loft. I had a tag-a-long little sister to escape from.

A few minutes later, I was standing in the feed loft looking out the door at the dusty barnyard 10 feet below. I tied the rope around my waist, tossed it over a rafter and pulled it tight. One foot slipped past the edge of the door and I froze. It was a long way down! Maybe I was not the hero type after all.

"What ya doin?" my little sister asked, looking up at me.

What to say? "I'm chickening out," certainly would not do. Wait a minute. This could be a great opportunity!

"Playing elevator," I said, looking down at her from the loft. "I lower myself to the ground then pull myself back up."

"I wanna try!"

"Well, I don't know. Mom might get mad. Remember swimming in the water trough?"

"I won't tell."

"OK. I'm getting tired of pulling myself anyway."

A moment later she was in the loft standing next to me. I tied the rope around her waist really tight. I could not have my sister slipping out half way down. That would definitely negate the "won't tell" pact!

"Ready?" I asked.

"Yep."

"OK, just step off . . . NO!" I screamed, too late.

She jumped out the door! The rope ripped through the skin on my hands, and I let it go, clenching my hands to make the pain stop. Then I heard a thud outside the door. I looked down, spotting my sister lying flat on her back with a cloud of dust rising around her. A moment later she shot up to her feet, screaming.

"I can't breathe! You killed me! You killed me!"

She raced for the gate with the rope trailing behind her. "MOOOMMM!!!!"

I was scared. My dad had waled on me for kicking the dog. I could only imagine what punishment killing my sister would bring! It was time to seek shelter in my secret fort in the hayloft.

I sat for hours inside that hot, dark little room built of

fresh-cut hay bales. When my stomach told me supper time was near, I began to rationalize the incident. My dad was upset about the dog because the dog could hunt. My sister could not hunt. In fact, I could not think of anything useful she did. Maybe dad would not be that upset. In any event, I was not about to die of hunger worrying about it.

My dad spotted me walking toward the house a few minutes later. "Where you been? Supper's waiting," he said, and then went into the house.

Wow. He must really love that dog! I took off running for the back door.

I froze in my tracks when I stepped into the kitchen. There she was sitting at the table, stuffing her face. She looked up at me and smiled an evil little smile. She had not told, but she could. Anytime. Anywhere. Just when it suited her best.

Funny thing about it was I never found out what she did with the rope. Years later I asked her about it, and she did not remember. I still wake up from nightmares seeing a noose made out of that rope—and hanging over my bed!

James and
sister Amy

CHAPTER SIX

Hodge Podge

Stories in a category of their own!

Rope Trick

by
Carole Spearin McCauley

It hung, swinging in the spring breeze, awaiting me—the girl. I named it Ronnie. My own Ronnie the Rope.

I stood on the path below the mountain's summit. We called this place the Ledge. Boy Scouts had climbed the immense oak tree and tied onto the largest limb the thick rope with its evenly spaced knots, thick as a man's fist.

Yet no one—until me—had swung the rope outward over the valley's nothingness. It's why I walked here, to fling off my shoes and socks, leap onto the thick knot and start to pump. First, back and forth over the path, for speed. Next, avoiding the cliff, to soar from the path's safety, outward bound into sheer air.

That's when Ronnie began to hum, to sing to me. Grasped between my hands, first tickling, and then chafing between my thighs and feet, Ronnie crooned to me, carried me where I needed to go. Ronnie's 60 feet of quivering, owl-brown length waited for me, caressed me. And I loved Ronnie's potent power to transport me. He had never failed me.

The path through the wooded mountains that held the rope tree was a longer way home from school, but I treasured it—compared with the boring road that wound hidden in the valley. I was 10 years old, so why rush home? My mother was always sick, fretting about her heart, making phone calls, ironing, getting dinner ready. The wide creases on her forehead reminded me of a cardboard carton—the rough-ridged inside part. My father arrived in his white shirt and either yawned or yelled. He and I used to read *Little Women* together—a gift from my grandmother—until he declared he was too tired.

That morning, for the first time, I stopped on my way to school because Mummy had a headache, Daddy spanked me, and I decided that I could miss a test on some math stuff I didn't understand.

And Ronnie's magic would make me forget.

Despite the earth's spring chill, I dropped my shoes and socks and ran to greet Ronnie. My callused feet hardly felt the path's sharp rocks. Then my fingers caressed Ronnie's length as if he were the teddy bear I was too old for.

The previous winter I had asked to ski, but there was no money for skis. The following spring I'd asked for ballet lessons, but there was no money for lessons, and "what can you do with it, anyway?" Same for horseback riding because "horses are dangerous and they smell—why can't you play softball with the other girls?" Yet my bratty baby brother got a train set. How was there money for that?

The week before I had tried to run away to my aunt who lives near Albany, but Mr. Kelly, the drugstore owner, caught me as I boarded the green Peter Pan bus—minus a suitcase.

With my bare feet I climbed onto Ronnie's bottom knot. I hugged him in my arms. Swinging straight off the narrow path, I clung tightly to Ronnie and began to pump outward. While my feet clasped the knot and my body accelerated, I knew that Ronnie could soar with me, like an eagle on thermals. That morning I didn't tire at all—I flexed the new muscles I felt. Blood rushed into them. That morning, too, the wind helped: updraft from valley and brook below lifted me the highest ever, cooled my cheeks, eased my chafed neck. I closed my eyes, opened my mouth, tasted the wind—leafy, mossy. On each outward arc, my straight brown hair streamed behind me. On each return, it covered my face and neck. I felt weightless, as if in a feather bed.

Ronnie's top knot, tied 60 feet above, creaked, singing to me. And I sang back, shouting to the valley's spring air, the brook's lady slippers, jack-in-the-pulpits, skunk cabbage, violets, wintergreen bark I had chewed the spearmint from. Now I sang to the weeping willows' sweeping skirts, the maples' and beeches' goldy-green. "Down in the valley, valley so high, hang your head over, hear the wind fly." I was the Evergreen World's daughter! Would my singing wake O.B. Joyful, the town drunk, sleeping it off in Peter's Cave above me?

That morning Ronnie was also my magic dragon. He had already flown me from cliff, ledge and dinky valley. *Suppose I ran away, became a trapeze artist in the circus? Couldn't I already climb and twist upside down on Ronnie, hanging by my arms? Never see my parents. Nor the bully-brat boys who knocked me into the marble curb that gashed my knee.* The red scar still showed the curb's black dirt. *No more arithmetic teacher's squinched face. No more "We-just-don't-understand-you-What's-the-matter-with-you?" stuff. But do they listen when I try to tell them? Hah! Do rocks fall upward?*

If I guided Ronnie to the right, I was on my way west toward Albany's green-domed capital building. How surprised my Aunt Almindine would be when I landed in her front yard. If I guided Ronnie eastward, I'd soar toward Boston, where my rich Aunt Juliette bought satin dresses with the money she could spend because she had no children. You bet! Best of all, as I pumped onward, sunward, Ronnie flew me south to the world's biggest city I had never seen except in my geography book: New York City!

I pumped faster, higher, underarms sweating. Wind rushed. Sun burst outward, up there in the clouds. Ronnie and I were cruising toward Albany. To lighten his load, I climbed farther up the rope, tilted my head back until I was dizzy, and then flung one arm and the opposite leg into space. I clung and swung, singing through the air. Sucked my breath in and out; nothing ever felt so good before—

"Carole! Git down from there. Now!"

"Tomboy! Show-off!" somebody else shouted.

And voices, half a universe away, knifed into my head, killing Ronnie's free pumping. I realized Ronnie's magic worked only when we were alone. I could soar forever then. But now— I twisted my neck, looked down. My vision blurred. Finally I forced my eyes to see, far below—goddam and a thousand fleas! Who were they? Those slugs with white faces and legs.

The sixth-grade nature class. One grade ahead of me. Nature was their Friday morning class, while I was skipping arithmetic. Now they stood on the path below, gawking. "You crazy, Carole? Call the police!" the teacher ordered. Some kid ran off, phoneward.

For an instant I imagined myself and Ronnie swooping across their path, blasting them all like bowling pins, straight into the valley. Without me to whip him onward, however, Ronnie slowed. Each arc swung, sang, shorter, stiller. Next I couldn't hear his music at all.

Parallel to the path, Ronnie dropped down to 6 feet, then 4 feet away from the group. Finally, only 2 feet. But with one grand pump and its arc, I could still have mowed them all down, and then soared again into the air—they would never have caught me.

At Ronnie's farthest pendulum point, 20 feet down the path, I hopped off, scooped up my shoes and ran for it. Get away!

"Carole!" they screamed.

Swinging back to center, Ronnie hung in the air, alone, behind me. Squelched for now.

Toffee Teeth

by
Glady Martin

I live in Canada, where Mackintosh Toffee is the rage. Made in Switzerland by Nestlé, the bar of toffee has always been one of my favorites, and I still eat it today.

When I was much, much younger, Mom would buy a bar of the sweet treat when our family went on car trips. Due to financial difficulties, the toffee was definitely a splurge; Mom would divide the bar among us four kids—my three younger brothers and me. We used to drive our parents beyond irritation with the famous question every parent loves to hear: "Are we there yet?" She would feed the toffee to us to keep us quiet during those trips. Chewing on the candy sealed our mouths shut nice and tight, so we truly were quiet! But what a succulent way to enjoy being quiet.

When I was eight years old, our family went to a friend's home for a big party. My aunt and uncle were there, too, and had brought their four little ones. That made eight kids. Add more kids from other families to the mix and the result was a whole pile of us running around, screaming and playing inside the very small home.

Tag was always one of our favorite inside games, which included teasing the uncles to the point that they chased us. We would let out high-pitched screeches when we got caught, yelling, "I give up! I give up!" We easily got under the skin of the adults by being so bratty. And we would sometimes bump into adults, accidentally spilling their drinks. That did not go over too well. Repeated orders of "Go outside to play!" fell on deaf ears—we were having too much fun inside.

Finally, the adults decided to give us money to go to the store—in other words, it was a bribe to go outside. Our uncle, who worked at a logging camp, brought out a jar of silver coins. We were beside ourselves with excitement, totally in awe at the sight of this "silver mine" and thoughts that we could buy out the store!

Well, as you can probably guess, we bought ourselves some Mackintosh Toffee. But this purchase was different. Each of us had enough money to buy a *whole* bar just for ourselves! No sharing necessary! Once we got home to show off our treasures, my daddy called me over to where he was sharing stories with a few of the other men.

"What ya got there, sweetie pie?" he asked me.

"I got my own toffee, Daddy . . . you want some?"

As he started to say "no," I shoved my toffee bar right into his mouth. His immediate reaction was to close his mouth, and he clamped down hard on my toffee bar.

I grabbed the one end of the bar sticking out of his mouth

and started shaking it back and forth. But it was lodged in his mouth.

I pleaded with him: "OK, Daddy, can I have it back now? Daddy? DAD! Give it back, please!"

Upset that Daddy wouldn't let go of my coveted candy, I gave the bar a good tug. To my horror, out came his teeth—they were cemented tight to my toffee bar! I held the bar, with his teeth stuck on the opposite end, in my hand for one frozen moment, absolutely shocked at what I saw. Then I screamed and threw the candy, teeth and all, to the floor. The teeth were actually dentures, but at only eight years old, I had never heard of dentures before. And when they broke into many pieces, I was even more upset. I ran from the room in a state of utter hysteria.

Dad quickly followed me, trying to explain that he had false teeth. But when I looked back and saw his naked gums enfolded with lips that seemed to cave into his mouth, I ran all the harder and yelled all the louder.

I never did take my toffee back that day. And whenever I eat a toffee bar, I remember how it made everyone laugh the day the "Toffee Teeth" story was born.

Perhaps Handel's
Water Music?

by
Jamie Miller

Every year, as reliable as the beginning of baseball and the
end of school, there was the highly anticipated—and equally
dreaded—recital by Mrs. Crane's piano students. We'd meet in
the Women's Club building and sit on metal folding chairs as we
waited our turn to play. The youngest were first, carefully plunk-
ing out one-hand melodies. Last were the older kids with their
flamboyant two-piano duets. I was an eighth grader. It would be
a long wait, and there I'd be in my wool suit—hot, dark, heavy,
tweedy and as rough inside as a full body pincushion.

I rebelled. "I don't wanna wear my suit!"

"But it looks so nice," my mother crooned. I was greatly
surprised and relieved, when—after seeing the distress in my
pleading face—she followed that statement with, "Well, OK,
you don't have to, I know that it's hot. You can wear slacks and
a white shirt instead."

So there sat the eighth graders in a neat row: me, Roger,

and then the irresistibly cute Marianne. Oh, how I longed to just speak to her! But I was painfully girl-shy.

We waited. And waited. And despite the fact that I should have felt comfortable in my cooler garb, I started to sense that I should have stopped in the restroom beforehand—and I began to sweat. We waited some more. I really had to pee, and we were only up to the fifth graders. Obviously, I couldn't get up and leave in the middle of a number; after all, what would the irresistible Marianne think? *Surely they'll have an intermission soon*, I prayed.

A sixth grader played Beethoven's entire *Fifth Symphony*. I clamped my legs together as the sweat continued to issue from my now-panicking body. A seventh grader played Wagner's complete *Ring Trilogy*. I began to leak. There was no turning back, and my tired muscles yielded. There was a trickle. There was a torrent. I heard people behind me lifting their feet.

A moment later, the seventh graders were done, and Mrs. Crane called on me to play. I shook my head, pleading with her through mortified eyes. She called again. "I can't," I whispered. She called yet again, and I surrendered. Maybe nobody would notice if I stood sideways to the audience, kept my thighs together and walked just from the knees down.

Perhaps I played *Chopsticks*. Perhaps Liszt. Whatever it was, they said I played brilliantly. The applause was generous and sustained. Now what? I didn't have an encore. Somehow, I would have to walk back to my chair. I stood, turned—thighs held tightly together—and looked down at the puddle on the piano bench. Thoughts raced through my brain: *Should I stop and clean it up? Would people notice what I was doing? Was my handkerchief still dry? What if Marianne was next? Are girls' dresses waterproof?*

"Let's have a little intermission," Mrs. Crane announced, finally. I stayed frozen, hoping people would forget I was there. Everyone graciously forgot, except my mother. She removed me from the scene of my crime as quickly as she could.

"I've never been so humiliated in my life!" she said as we drove away. "If you'd worn your suit, nobody would have noticed." A practical idea, I thought, but still I wondered, *Could wool have held that much pee?*

And so we fled, leaving behind in ruins both my career as a concert pianist and my fantasy romance with the lovely Marianne.

Rocking the Red

by
Lisa Hemrich

From the tips of her pointed red fingernails to the tops of her frosty blue eyelids, my Aunt Nonnie was the queen of bling in 1977—and she was an Avon lady. *It didn't get any cooler than that*, I thought. I longed to flash my bright red talons and color my face like a rainbow. To a five-year-old whose mama thought wearing ruffled panties and lace socks with your Mary Jane shoes counted as accessorizing, the boxes of Avon samples stashed under Nonnie's bed were like Disneyland and Heaven all rolled into one.

After every overnight visit to my Aunt Nonnie's, I came home with tiny tubes of lipstick in every color of the rainbow. The red ones were my favorite, but there wasn't much I could do with them except draw pictures on my hand—it wasn't like I could wear lipstick to my elementary school! So I counted and sorted and organized the tiny tubes and bottles and dreamed of the day when I could paint my face and nails, just like Aunt Nonnie.

In my heart I knew I could be a master makeup artist, and one day I got my chance. Mom's sister came over and brought my baby cousin Andrea. Her blond curls and blue eyes were screaming for some bling, and I had the tools and abilities to fix her up. I don't know what Mom and my aunt thought I was doing to entertain a one-year-old in my room for half an hour, but they didn't bother to check on us.

When I paraded Andrea through the living room, dressed in my best doll clothes and made up like a true Vegas showgirl, I thought they'd be impressed. And I thought they would even tell me I'd earned the right to wear at least the light pink stuff to school. Boy, was I wrong.

Furious doesn't quite describe the reaction I got as I stood there with my pretty little cousin. All of my carefully inventoried samples instantly became the possession of my mother. My life was over—summer was coming and I was sure I would've been able to paint my toenails red until school started in the fall. Now my supplies were gone, and I was left with plain pink and white toes.

My inner diva came through a few days later in the form of a brilliant idea. My lipstick and nail polish were gone, but my school supplies' closet was well-stocked. I had markers—lots and lots of RED markers. I tried out several on a piece of paper, looking for just the right shade to go with my last-day-of-school outfit. I finally found the perfect brightly saturated shade of blood red. The marker was big with a wide angled tip, and it was hard to control on my tiny five-year-old toes. I got a little on my skin, but that just made my toenails look longer. Really, if you just glanced at them and I kept my feet moving, you wouldn't have known it wasn't a professional pedicure.

My mom knew, though. In fact, she screamed when I went waltzing through the kitchen in my favorite sandals, rocking those red toes. Turns out her permanent red marker had been missing for a while, and she hadn't thought to look in my marker box. While washable markers come off skin in a few washings, a permanent red Marks-a-Lot is not intended to be so easily removed.

So off I went to my last day of kindergarten, refusing to admit I'd made a mistake, wearing my new summer sandals and looking like someone had cut my toenails with a jagged butcher knife.

Now if you'll excuse me, I need to go work on my toes— the sparkles are coming loose!

Why Did Cynthia Slap Me?

by
Terri Elders

Looking back, I'm certain I only wanted us all to get better acquainted. I'd skipped third grade, so was both younger and smaller than my classmates. By sixth grade, I had no close friends other than my neighbor, Beth. She was a shorty, too, so we had something in common.

I didn't know how to chat with classmates. I'd ask if somebody liked to read *Nancy Drew* or followed the Dodgers, but if the answer turned out to be "no," the conversation died right there. I'd never been part of the inside crowd, never got nominated for class officer or picked for the cheerleading squad, never been popular or cool. But I wanted to know the kids who sat near me in class. I felt like I was caged up with total strangers.

At the start of the year our teacher, Miss Barnes, made clear her views about slam books.

"Some of you might think it's funny to write mean things

about your classmates," she'd said, glowering as if we were all heartless losers, "but your comments can be harsh and hurtful. In this classroom, slam books will be contraband."

She wrote the word on the blackboard. "Who can tell me what contraband means?"

Gary raised his hand. We girls swiveled our heads. Our collective megawatt smiles would have blinded him had he bothered to glance around. Instead, he gazed straight ahead.

"It's something prohibited, Miss Barnes, something illegal."

The girls nodded. The boys rolled their eyes.

"Very good." Miss Barnes wrote "prohibit" on the board then awarded Gary a smile. I didn't blame her. Any female would feel compelled to beam at the sight of him. Anybody who claimed that perfection was unattainable had never laid eyes on Gary.

"In Room 22, I prohibit slam books and chewing gum," Miss Barnes reiterated. "They distract from the learning process."

I froze guiltily mid-chew, clamped my jaws shut and glanced at Beth in the seat to my left. After school we rendez-voused by the school entrance to walk home together.

"My sister had a slam book last year," I confided. "She let me read it. Nobody wrote anything mean in it. It was just about hobbies and pets and fun stuff. So I bought a spiral notebook, and I thought maybe we could decorate it and pass it around, make a getting-to-know-you book. But you heard what Miss Barnes said."

Beth shook her head, her auburn ponytail swishing from shoulder to shoulder. "Oh, we're not bullies. We wouldn't invite anybody to write anything mean. I'll come over after dinner and we can make up some questions. Sounds like an awesome idea."

That evening we sneaked a plate of my mom's butterscotch cookies into my bedroom. We perched on the bed and clipped out pictures from magazines to make a collage for the cover of my getting-to-know-you notebook. We even glued on swatches of red and blue satin ribbon and some silver sequins left over from my old Halloween princess costume.

"It looks pretty glamorous," Beth said, helping herself to the last cookie. We'd left the title box blank, but now I plucked up a purple felt pen and wrote, "Welcome to Terri and Beth's *Glam* Book."

It took us nearly an hour to finish entering our questions at the top of each page. *What will you be when you grow up? What national park would you like to see? What's your hobby? Who's your favorite superhero? What's your favorite subject?*

"I wonder what Gary will say his favorite subject is," Beth said.

I laughed. "Has there ever been a cooler guy than Gary? He just rocks."

"I've got another question." Beth giggled. "We could ask, 'Who is your secret crush and why?'"

"That's great! Do you think anybody will answer?"

"All the girls will say Gary."

"Well, there must be some other boys that girls admire." I stared at the bedspread, pretending to be deep in thought.

"Oh, right! No doubt!" Beth and I collapsed with laughter and nearly fell off my bed.

The next day, I toted the book to school and handed it to Cynthia at nutrition break.

"We're not supposed to have slam books," she said, pushing it back to me. Like Beth and me, Cynthia was an outsider. A little chunky, she wore thick glasses. She lived near school, so she walked home for lunch. She never accepted our invitations to join us in after-school activities, but we liked her nonetheless.

"It's not! You'll see. It's a *glam* book. All the questions are innocent. Nothing naughty."

"OK, then." Cynthia slipped the book inside her jacket. "It might be fun since it's not a slam book."

All week the book circulated among our classmates. Soon nearly everybody had taken a turn writing in it. People started to approach Beth and me during lunch.

"Hey, girlfriend, thanks for making that amazing book."

"Wow, I enjoyed filling in the answers."

"I'd no clue you collected koala bears! So do I!"

On Friday, things suddenly changed.

"Uh oh. Here comes Cynthia and she looks mad." Beth crinkled her forehead.

Cynthia walked over, her face white. She dropped the book in front of me. "Thanks for nothing," she said. Then she crossed the room to the table where all the cool kids sat and slapped Gary hard across his cheek.

Everybody silently stared as she turned on her heel and left. Gary sat still, looking dazed as he rubbed his cheek.

After school Gary stopped me at the school entrance.

"Why did Cynthia slap me?"

"I don't know," I said.

"I think it has something to do with that book you're circulating."

I pulled it out of my backpack and opened it up to the sign-in page. The last person to sign in had written in capital letters, GARY.

"I never signed your book. Call it what you want, but I heard Miss Barnes warn against slam books. My parents would kill me if I got into trouble over something as silly as a slam book."

Together, we flipped through the pages. On the last one with the question about secret crushes, the person masquerading as Gary had scribbled, "Cynthia . . . hot, hot, hot."

Gary glared at me. "I never wrote that."

I believed him. I just shook my head.

I never found out who pretended to be Gary. Sometimes I suspected it was Beth, but she denied it. I apologized to Cynthia for having brought the book to school. She stared at me, and then shuffled away.

I realized then that Miss Barnes had been right. At least one person had thought it fun to say mean things. Certainly whoever had written that Cynthia was hot planned for that to get a big laugh at her expense.

When Beth and I put together that book, I never dreamed that it could have such an effect on somebody else. Cynthia never spoke to either of us again. The next year she changed schools.

Gary continued to be friendly, but I don't think he ever forgave me. He never would have hurt anybody's feelings.

I never came up with a truthful answer to his question. I really don't know why Cynthia slapped him. She should have known he was too nice to be the culprit.

It's me she should have slapped.

Oh, Those Tangled Webs

by
Kathe Campbell

Plunged into the Great Depression of the early 1930s, my mother nevertheless developed a flair for humor, and the perpetual humming of lovely tunes defined her. She was no bigger than a minute, a born cook, gardener and hostess. Every morning she floated down the stairs perfectly turned out, with colorful earrings to match perky house dresses. She played the piano and organ at our church, lived for lunch and weekly bridge with the girls, and sang contralto with the St. Cecilia Society. But mostly she was a stay-at-home peach of a mom.

While changing sheets in my bedroom one morning, Mom spotted an unfamiliar shiny red barrette perched on my dresser. Knowing my passion for colorful hair clips, she casually asked where this one had come from. "Oh, I don't know—from one of my drawers," I chirped, as my heart raced and my face flushed a revealing red.

She'd have probably accepted that as God's truth if the packaging and price tag weren't leering up at her from my waste basket. I sensed my undoing when she drew all of her 5-foot-2-inch frame up tall and judicious as the interrogation began. "Are you sure you weren't playing with this barrette in Woolworth's, and maybe you forgot to put it back when you left?" Her soft voice left a gaping opportunity for me to come clean.

Sir Walter Scott nailed it when he cautioned, "Oh what a tangled web we weave when first we practice to deceive. And this eight-year-old tomboy was starting to weave a pretty tangled web.

"Oh, now I remember, this is Sissy's barrette. She said I could wear it while their family goes on vacation." My web had trapped the fib of the century. I don't know why I was unable to allow myself Mom's generous pardon, but my mind was awhirl, caught up in a frenzy over thoughts of the previous day.

Mom rarely parted with a precious nickel for a candy bar, and yesterday had been no exception. Never absconding with coins from her pocketbook—because mothers knew their change purses by heart—this larcenous little soul sat on the back porch pouting, trying to come up with a plan on how to get money for the store.

I don't recall just when the great light went on, but the abrupt flash launched me straight into my father's den and his prized coin collection. I liberated a couple of 1913-D Indian head nickels, and Sissy and I skipped off to purchase a sack of bulk chocolate at Woolworth's. Without one red cent left between us, the latest hair fashions evoked such ineffable longings that I felt driven straight into the arms of the devil. I stole the barrette.

My list of misdemeanors was growing blacker by the minute, and all the while I swore like a trooper about that wretched red barrette. My mother was on a mission, however, and masterfully executed the third degree twice more that afternoon, relentlessly chipping away at wringing the truth out of me.

Would I sit alone in my room consoling myself with hidden chunks of chocolate, tangling one sorry story atop another, or would I confess? Regarding the latter, not on your life. I was one stubborn kid. How I wished my mother would give it up so I could go outdoors and play! But playtime was not on this lady's agenda. She had a different game in mind—the waiting game. She was waiting for the truth, and I was waiting for a spanking.

Petrifying kids of my generation, sharp wallops with green willow switches or the pancake turner were not considered corporal punishment back in the dark ages. Would I be sporting little red badges of courage across the back of my legs? The fact was, echoes of woeful wails filled balmy breezes up and down our street as bottoms were regularly paddled over an irate mother's lap. Even at school, wooden rulers across derrieres and knuckles were routine in that godawful inner sanctum called the Principal's Office.

Mother smiled and kissed Dad at the door that evening, and then called me to dinner. During grace I felt such remorse and was so nauseous I could barely look at my plate, but I was greatly relieved when she didn't snitch to Dad. While she washed the dishes and I dried, sharp glances pierced my very soul—she was still silently goading me to fess up. Beautiful as she was, those pursed lips and foreboding stare repelled my guilty glances.

Rather than copping a plea with Dad, I finally wandered into the bathroom where Mom was applying a fresh face. A sudden flood of tears poured out, washing me free as I fell into her arms to come clean. "Sorry, Mommy, sorry," I sobbed as she held me tightly, lecturing honesty until at long last I felt sweet kisses on my cheek.

I thought about my dear mother who bent over backward to turn me out well—who told me often how much she loved me—just before rebounding chocolate spawned a retched comeuppance around midnight.

Upon entering Woolworth's the following afternoon, I returned the barrette with a chagrinned apology while the stern-faced manager issued a long sermon on the evils of stealing.

That summer of 1939 remains vivid after 70 years, for my mom had taught me the art of good parenting. She is still the endless sweet humming in my heart, full of comfort, happiness and being. I may forget the words, but I'll always remember the tunes from my peach of a mom as they waft their way through the tangled webs of my past.

Kathe (right) and her mom

Just Ducky

by
Maureen Bureson

I was six the first time I baby-sat my little brother, Tom, all by myself. He was still in diapers. My older brother was assisting the priest at Mass, and both my parents wanted to attend. Since they could not afford a baby sitter—and Tom was sleeping—they decided it was probably OK to leave him with me.

I felt so grown up! I could do whatever I wanted! I considered the possibilities. I ignored the doll I got for my birthday, derisively labeling it "girl stuff," and considered the book Dad was reading to me the day before. My ruminations were rudely interrupted, though, by a suddenly wide-awake—and crying—baby brother. He was supposed to stay asleep. *I'll just bring him his teddy bear to play with in his crib so I can get back to my book,* I thought, figuring that would take care of the situation.

But Tom shoved the teddy bear away. I tried his truck, his ball, everything I could think of to calm him, but he was having none of these distractions—he wanted his mommy. I didn't know what else to do, so I decided I'd just take him to church. But first I had to get ready.

I hated dresses, but since Mom always wore a dress to church, I reluctantly concluded that I should, too. Unfortunately, the dress I selected buttoned in the back, and I was unable to button it by myself. *Oh well,* I figured, *it will just have to stay open.* It never occurred to me that I could choose a different dress.

As we approached the front door, ready to make our way to church, Tom cried even louder and kept pulling me back into the living room. Finally, he broke away from me and ran to his ducky. Ducky rolled on wheels and quacked loudly as he moved along. I hoped that ducky would satisfy him, that I wouldn't have to take him to church, and that I could get back to my book. After playing with it for a few minutes, however, he started screaming for Mommy again. So I took his hand and headed for the door once more, with him still crying and making it clear that he was not leaving the house without his noisy toy. At that point, to shut him up, I let him take his ducky.

I chose to take the shortcut to church, a path on the side of a mountain away from streets and sidewalks. Though I was going the fastest way, it was not the easiest way for Tom. Walking on the path was difficult while he wore his diaper. He kept trying to pull it off, but as he wasn't wearing anything else, I kept telling him he had to wear it. He didn't agree. It was a constant battle as we continued along the path toward the church, and it ended in a stalemate. When we arrived at the church, his diaper was halfway down.

We entered the church right at the consecration of the Eucharist, the most solemn moment in the ceremony. The only sound when we entered was my big brother ringing a bell as the priest lifted the bread. I took Tom's hand, and as we walked up the center aisle, ducky quacked along behind us. The unmistakable quacking sound, joined with the sound of the bell, alerted the congregation that this would be no ordinary Mass.

When the priest turned to see what was going on, a big grin broke out on his face before he returned his attention to the altar to raise the cup. I saw Mom and Dad sitting way up front in the first row. I was surprised when Dad—upon seeing us—immediately turned back toward the altar and looked straight ahead, as if he didn't know us. Mom, though, took one look, and with a horrified expression on her face, whisked us out of church and took us to the car.

She didn't say a word, and I was so relieved that Tom had stopped his carrying on. Even though I know I had done the right thing that day, I never understood why it was years before I ever got to baby-sit my little brother again.

Maureen and her older brother

One Man's Trash

by
Banjo Bandolas

Today's high-tech mountain bikes are sleek, complicated machines that carry a higher price tag than my grandfather's first mortgage. In a simpler time, when great nomadic herds of hippies roamed the earth, one speed was all you needed and suspension stiffness depended on how much air you'd put in the tires at the gas station. Those were the days when Bob Dylan and the beater bike reigned supreme.

For a kid, there's an advantage to riding a beater rather than a store-bought bike. Beater bikes were worthless. If you walked up to someone and offered to trade a beater bike straight across for a half-eaten candy bar, they'd probably want to think about it, and then politely decline. Since the bike represented little or no value, parents couldn't care less what happened to it. My beater was the first thing I'd ever owned that was completely mine.

This is the story of how Silver and I met.

It was a beautiful spring day in North Carolina. The scent of flowering magnolia and dogwood filled the air, and a fresh bamboo fishing pole dangled over my shoulder. I think I might've even been whistling at the time—it was a very Opie Taylor moment.

As I approached my favorite fishing hole, the glint of something shiny at the bottom of a deep drainage ditch caught my eye. Lying in the weeds, partially covered with debris, was a bike. I slid down the bank for a closer inspection.

Not bad, I thought, grabbing the frame and wrestling it from the weeds. It was an old one-speed Raleigh with two flat tires and a rusted snarl for a chain. Someone had spray painted the frame silver—logo and all—but other colors peeked out from various chips and scratches. It was just about the most beautiful thing I'd ever seen. Being a fan of *Lone Ranger* reruns from the 1960s, and having a relatively limited imagination, I immediately dubbed my new steed "Silver."

After numerous attempts, I finally managed to drag the big bike from the ditch. I kneeled next to it, plucking grass from the spokes while I caught my breath. All thoughts of fishing evaporated instantly. I tossed my pole into the bushes and started the long push home, babying the abused bike over every log and rock. *No sense adding to its injuries.* When I got home, I carefully washed it then began the learning experience of fixing my first bike. I didn't have any money or help, so I did what I could with what I had.

Mechanical challenges had never daunted me. I'd grown up taking things apart and figuring how they worked. Of course they didn't always go back together as easily as they came apart, or even work afterward, but those experiences gave me the confidence I needed to tackle the job at hand.

The chain ended up soaking in my mother's good bucket under a couple of quarts of Dad's motor oil. Both tires were cracked and dry, but there weren't any rips or big holes in them, so I figured they'd work for a while.

I wasn't as lucky with the tubes—they had more holes than a strainer! And who knows how many more I made while prying the tires from the rims with two big screwdrivers. I found an old patch kit in the garage and using what I remembered from watching older boys fix their tires, I went for it. I roughed up the rubber around the holes with the metal lid, and after smearing glue over and around the hole, I applied the patch. After that, I touched a lighted match to it. Vulcanizing those patches on was the first constructive thing I'd ever done with matches! When the job was done, I had used every patch and drop of glue in the kit and the tire tubes were lumpy with thick patches of every shape and size, but they held air and I was proud of my first official patch job.

Working the chain over was a messy operation. Once all the joints were broken loose, I grabbed a wire brush and tried to clean off the rust. I learned that a chain is a hard thing to hold down. After using about every outside surface and position I could imagine, I got the chain relatively rust-free. But our cement driveway was now decorated with a Spirograph of oily chain prints, framed with rusty orange handprints and spray.

Reconstruction went relatively smoothly, even though my entire body was one big mechanic's rag of stains from head to toe. I stood for a moment, smiling to myself, as I admired my handiwork.

Silver was a very ugly bike. The right handlebar, graced with a red grip, was bent slightly higher than the left white grip. Long deep scratches and dents covered the frame, proud scars from past battles with bone-breaking obstacles. The inflated tires and oil-dripping chain begged me to test them. Silver was ready for his maiden voyage.

I still remember that first ride. I couldn't straddle the frame in the upright position so—to allow room for my personality—I had to hold the frame at either the 10- or 2-o'clock position. After taking a deep breath, I threw the bike and myself into an upright stance, stabbing blindly for the pedal with my push foot. Having ridden larger bikes before, I knew the trick was to get the bike moving before gravity took over and I fell into a graceless heap.

The bike and I teetered for a moment as I pulled on the M-shaped handlebars and bore down on the pedal with all the power a boy could muster. The wheels slowly began to inch forward. Before I'd reached the end of the driveway, I had my balance and I shot out onto the black asphalt road. Peddling was difficult at first; my toes barely touched the worn rubber pedal at the bottom of the stroke. A rhythmic *bip bip bip . . . bip bop . . . bip bip bip* sound came from the tires as the tread hopped from patch to patch.

Up to this point, I had avoided messing with the handbrakes, instead focusing on fixing the bike's major problems. *That would be a puzzle for another day. How important are brakes anyway?* I had reasoned to myself. When I squeezed the brake levers, they jumped and screeched like a cat caught in a car door, but they stopped me . . . eventually.

I rode around for hours. It was a wonderful day. The birds sang sweeter, the grass was greener, and I had a bike. Opportunities for the coming summer of exploration seemed limitless. Adventures that would leave lesser bikes on the scrap heap wouldn't scare me and Silver. His bad paint job covered a heavy solid steel frame that could take punishment. I just knew he'd carry me into any godforsaken hellhole I chose to explore and back out again, without fail.

Plans for my first official road trip were already forming in my head as I rattled into my yard and wheeled around back. Our car sat in the driveway and I was anxious to show Dad my new bike.

Rounding the back corner of the house, I saw Mom and Dad standing by the garage. They were shaking their heads as they surveyed the environmental disaster the driveway had become. Their smoldering eyes fixated upon me as I rolled up with a huge smile on my face. I came to a stop in front of them with a screech that made them jump back in alarm. Then, I balanced for a split second, expertly stuck my right foot out, fell over and caught myself. Before they had time to collect their wits or open their mouths, I launched into my news.

"Lookatmynewbike!Ifounditinaditch!Ifixeditallbymy-selfanditworksandeverything." I took a ragged breath and finished, "Pretty cool, huh?"

Mom and Dad looked at each other and sighed. The fire was doused.

"It's a beautiful bike, sweetie!" Mom said. Reaching out to

ruffle my dirty hair, she hesitated and thought better of it. She turned to Dad, "You owe me a bucket. I'm going to get supper on the table. Good luck getting that gunk off him—you'll probably have to use turpentine."

Dad looked down at me and I smiled up at him, displaying every tooth I had.

"Nice bike, son," he said, choking a little on something. "You must have worked really," he paused, looking around at the scattered tools and puddles of oil, "really hard on it. Let's go to the garage and see if we can scrape some of that mess off you. Maybe we'll find a boy under all that grease." We paused at his open toolbox on the way to the garage. "I think it's about time we fixed you up your own toolbox," he said, looking down at the spilled contents. Then with a little sigh, "Looks like you're gonna need it."

Ugly as that old bike was, I wouldn't have traded him for any shiny new Schwinn or European 10-speed. You never forget your first and in that private place in my heart where all my firsts are stored, there's a beat-up, piece-of-crap bike called Silver.

You Did WHAT?!

Crazy, ridiculous, even dangerous
tales of mischief!

Shagging is Hard

by
Kendall Roderick

The hallway carpet leading into the school cafeteria was an emerald green mixed with puke brown and sky blue. I imagined that without the puke color, it might have been mildly pleasant.

I was meeting Sarah, who had been my best friend for years, for lunch. My mother had always begged me not to hang out with such a bad influence, the girl who had taught me curse words in fifth grade and who bragged about watching R-rated movies. She liked to dye her hair and wear clothes that were undesirably bright. I knew I was still desperately behind in high school knowledge, and Sarah was the only one brave enough to explain the dirty jokes and the strange words that passed through the hall daily. But my mom didn't understand all of that.

We took dance classes together: swing, balboa, salsa, our first shag class—another form of swing dancing. It was what we did every day after school at a semi-shady downtown hippie club where we were the youngest participants. We had made college friends there and talked about it regularly. We figured it couldn't hurt being friends with older guys. Swing dancing was undeniably our thing, but shag was something new and exciting and, as it turned out, also very hard. I had pretty much fallen over my own feet the whole night, but one of our college friends, Ray, had taken to it quite nicely. He had danced like there was nothing to it.

When I entered the cafeteria, I saw Sarah propped up against the side wall on the far end. As usual, she was picking at her food like a bird and enjoying laughs with a large group of strangers. I sat down next to her, scooching her over. Our shoulders bumped awkwardly as we tried to get comfortable on the metal park bench. I usually started the conversations. I was talkative but never one to talk during classes, so when I could talk, I couldn't contain myself.

"Last night was pretty fun," I said. Sarah didn't look up, but popped a grape in her mouth and gave me a funny face. "I thought it was really difficult."

Sarah again said nothing, but shrugged slightly.

"Everyone seemed to be having a hard time except for Ray."

"Oh, I didn't notice," Sarah said, still not paying attention. She was different at school, more popular. She had more friends than I could count, but for me, it was pretty much just her.

"You didn't? Ray was shagging like it was nothing. It just seemed so natural to him."

Another girl at the table lightly coughed and eyed the rest of the people, who were all now paying close attention. I couldn't imagine why.

"You didn't think so?" I asked Sarah, confused on why she was eyeing the others as if they were participants in a game show. I crossed my arms in front of me, ready to defend myself, but also intimidated by the onlookers with their sudden intense interest. "Well, I think he's great at shagging."

Sarah lurched forward in an uncontrollable laugh, her body leaning into the metal picnic table as her hair lightly grazed over her food.

"What? Truthfully, Sarah!" I lightly smacked her arm. "He was the only one I shagged with where it felt right. He's really good at it."

Sarah motioned with her hand as if she were a football coach trying to call a timeout. From the snickers on the other side of the table, I'm certain my face was turning a soft shade of scarlet, but I didn't know what I had done wrong. Sarah had managed to say "Stop!" in a gurgle-type cough that mixed with her laughter, though my nervousness always made me talk more.

"Didn't you shag with him?" My tone reflected my irritation and a slightly higher volume that brought more listeners.

Sarah caught the new onlookers' eyes and magically, her laughing stopped. "Kendall, seriously?"

"What?"

Sarah leaned over, cupping her hands around her mouth to form a tunnel to my ear. She then whispered, and the faint scarlet that my face had become earlier turned a distasteful color of burning flames. I was mortified because, according to Sarah, "shag" meant sex, and to high school students, it certainly meant sex in all instances. My mind played back through our conversation, and it didn't sound like innocent dance talk. I left the cafeteria, following the path of nasty puke-colored carpet, listening to the giggles disappear in the background.

Kendall

Kendall (left) and Sarah

Bombs Away!

by
Jerry W. Baker

In 1957, life was much simpler. The Dallas population was a mere 500,000. Most people that I knew lived in two-bedroom, 1,500-square-foot homes and owned only one car. Our family was no exception.

Like my friends, in addition to going to school and playing sports, we all worked part-time jobs. There was little time left for a social life. I got up at the crack of dawn, or sometimes earlier, to throw my paper route, returned home about 6:30 A.M. to grab a quick breakfast, and then caught a ride to school with friends.

The last period of school was sports—track, baseball or just working out in general, before catching a ride home. I'd grab a bite to eat and rush to finish any homework. At 7 P.M., I drove the family auto to my dad's store a few blocks away. That's where I would sweep the wooden floors, restock shelves, clean the stock room and anything else Dad could conjure up to keep me busy right up to closing time.

There was no slouching around when you worked for Dad. He was a child of the Depression and a WWII Marine Corps veteran. He fought on Okinawa and other places throughout the South Pacific, but he didn't talk about it. Dad was soft spoken, but fair. He drew a line and let you know what the rules were. But one rule prevailed above all others—you did not lie!

In our modest neighborhood, only a mere three blocks from my home, lived a girl named Peggy. I passed her corner house every evening heading to Dad's store. Peggy was really pretty, and I kind of liked her. In the summer, she was often in the front yard and I'd stop to visit if I wasn't running late for work. Dad didn't tolerate me being late for work.

One cool autumn evening, yours truly was headed to work with a cherry bomb in his shirt pocket—a leftover firecracker from the Fourth of July. These cherry bombs were particularly nasty. They were slightly smaller than a golf ball and crammed full of powder and BBs. My plan was to toss it into Peggy's yard to impress her.

It was dark when I pulled up in front of her house. With the cherry bomb in hand, I lit the fuse with the car's cigarette lighter and threw the cherry bomb out the driver's-side window. I was flabbergasted when it bounced back and landed on the bench seat, just inches from me. The damn car window was still UP!

The next second or two seemed like fast forward, slow motion and freeze frame all rolled into one. In a state of sheer panic, I stupidly attempted to exit through the passenger door, not the driver's door. With my back arched, I struggled to climb right over the top of the bomb to reach the passenger door when the cherry bomb exploded! The noise was deafening, and the entire car filled with smoke.

I threw open the passenger door to dive out, and then realized the car was still in drive, creeping across the intersection. Fortunately, no cars were coming, but I now was on the passenger side of the car. I guided it to a stop with my left hand on the steering wheel, my head partially out of the passenger door trying to breathe, while stomping around with my left foot until I found the brake pedal. Once the car was in park, I stumbled out and stood numb, attempting to figure out what the hell had just happened.

Still in shock, I staggered around to the driver's side to survey the damage. Opening the door, I couldn't believe my eyes. In the middle of the front seat was a hole larger than a softball. Material from the hole was plastered all over the dashboard, and the headliner had dozens of holes in it. Not to mention, the glass on nearly every gauge—the speedometer, radio, clock and more—either had BB holes, pits or cracks. It was then I thought seriously about leaving the country, for Dad was sure to kill me. And I still hadn't discovered the hole blown in the rear of my Levi's and my scorched underwear.

I had no choice but to continue to the store. That three-minute drive felt like an hour. I pulled into a parking space, took a few deep breaths, and went inside. I felt it was far safer to break the news to Dad inside where other people lingered about.

Honestly, I don't have a clue as to what I told Dad or even how I said it. I'm certain I spoke rapidly, probably stammered a few times, and that my voice was a couple of octaves higher than normal.

Once I confessed, the two of us marched outside to see the damage. I stayed well back while Dad made his inspection. He then turned toward me and started to speak. I had decided beforehand that whatever his reaction was, I fully deserved what I had coming. I braced myself. Amazingly, Dad suddenly turned his back to me and said, "I'll let you know when it's paid for. Until then, there will be no paychecks for you." Indeed, it was an extremely long time until I saw another paycheck.

The incident was never discussed in the confines of our home, and no one outside of the family was ever told. I could only assume my parents were humiliated to discover their son was so downright stupid.

I ran into Peggy at a high school gathering a few years ago and told her about the cherry-bomb incident. She never knew. And she laughed so hard, she started to cry. After 50 years, I was embarrassed all over again. And will be again and again, as each of you read my story. Please don't laugh too hard.

The family car and Jerry

The Date

by

Dawn Keeley Caunce

Ninth grade. There I was on a date with the beloved and utterly gorgeous Frankie Smith. I was the envy of the school in our quaint English village of Preston.

Frankie did the usual yawn and stretch to try for a naughty grope. Unfortunately for him, I was engrossed in the movie. *Oh no, don't go back in! Everyone knows you shouldn't go back into the room!* I thought to myself as I watched the action on the screen and ate my popcorn. Frankie leaned in and a pungent whiff of cheap drugstore cologne hit me head-on. He was now staring at me intently. How was I to know that meant he was going to stick his tongue down my throat? Seconds later, as he went in for the kill, our noses clashed. Mortified, we parted and tried again. Our lips eventually met. I closed my eyes embracing the moment . . . *tender . . . hmmm . . . a taste of Camel cigs . . . nice.*

The music from the movie was building, echoing round the theatre. I peeked at the screen—*Run! Run faster!* Frankie's tongue went darting in, round and round, quite off-putting, really. Something caught my attention—my school nemesis and her cronies just two rows down. She kept turning round and giggling. *Ah! Jealous cow.*

Finally he came up for air. *Phew!* I was beginning to feel like a fish. I could sense something slithering up my leg, hitching up my skirt. *Damn! Why did I wear this?* Perhaps Ma was right; a leather mini did give off the wrong signals. I swiped at Frankie's hand. "Watch the movie," I mouthed, kissing him sweetly on his nose.

No! Hit him again! Whack him! Everyone knows he won't be dead! Frankie's hand was wandering again. Jeez, this lad had some moves, and they were getting to be quite annoying. *Don't lean over him, daft cow!* The music built to a crescendo, heart pounding, shuffling forward, I gripped Frankie's hand—first, because I was trying to stop him playing *Itsy Bitsy Spider* up my thigh, and second, it was scary stuff, this film!

I closed my eyes and turned slightly away from the screen. I couldn't look. "Arggh!" I screamed. Frankie's hand had migrated to my boob just as the psycho grabbed the girl's leg. As I screamed and jumped, popcorn flew out of the tub everywhere and the whole auditorium—including Frankie—joined my shrieks. Security rushed in and shone a flashlight over to where we were sitting. I was, however, not there anymore; instead, I was 2 feet in the air and about to come down with a thud. I landed on the inclined cinema seat. *Ah! My tush-bone!*

The cinema crowd erupted in laughter. There I was sitting bolt upright, my top all askew with my left boob exposed for all to see. *Gee, thanks, Frankie. And why is this pervy guard still flashing that light on me?* Yes, you could say that it was a night to remember, especially since Frankie decided I was far too frigid for his liking and dumped me there and then, leaving me—disheveled—in a flood of tears.

Of course I was the talk of the school for a quite a while after that, earning myself the nickname "Fried Eggs" thanks to my nemesis, who I know is still jealous of my make-out date with Frankie. In addition to being dumped that night, I was also banned from the cinema for making too much noise and causing unnecessary upset to the audience.

There was, however, something good that came out of that night's fiasco. I got to watch movies in peace for a good long time thereafter—in a different theatre!

Dawn,
then (above)
and now

Snake Boy

by
Banjo Bandolas

My family has a very deep, very dark secret. A secret that, to my family's complete and utter dismay, I'm about to reveal to you. It's a secret that no one mentions in polite company and one that has caused my family years of trepidation and cost thousands of dollars in therapy.

That secret is my obsession with snakes. I mean, I *really* like snakes.

I know what you're thinking; snakes ... Deep South ... religion is going to poke its head up out of the pine straw any second. To be fair, when most people think of the snake-handling religions—and when are they truly far from anyone's mind?—the Deep South and Appalachia do top the list. Though I've never so much as passed the time of day with a serpent-handling preacher, or set foot in one of their churches, I do admire and have committed to memory a scripture from the book of Mark that is central to their beliefs: "They shall take up serpents; and if they drink any deadly thing, it shall not hurt them; they shall lay hands on the sick, and they shall recover." ~ Mark 16:17-18

Now how could anyone hate a critter that can do that for you? I don't see anyone attributing such power to anything else in the animal kingdom. So it's with pride that I proclaim I somehow seem to be missing the gene that makes most other people fearful of these villains of Eden.

Maybe I got it from my Grandma Rose. She never seemed afraid of snakes, but unlike me, she hated them with a passion. If you were an unwary reptile who inadvertently crossed my grandma's path when she had a hoe within reach, you'd find yourself hacked into a dozen pieces before you could hiss, "Pardon me."

I remember the first snakes I ever caught. Yes, plural. I was six years old and my family and I were enjoying an outing at a local lake, which included fishing. The catfish weren't biting, and I grew bored with bobber watching, so while the others visited, I wandered on up the hill for a little exploration. I hadn't gone too far when I saw a beautiful black and yellow snake coiled in the dry grass, watching me. (Later I learned it was an Eastern king snake, and it's said to kill and eat rattlesnakes.) I don't know where I learned it, but I instinctively knew how to maneuver around and pin its head down with the lightning quick reflexes only young boys seem to possess. I lifted up the snake, extending as high as my little arm could reach. The snake was so long that a substantial portion of it remained twisting on the ground.

As I admired the king snake's alternating black and yellow scales, movement on the ground caught my eye. Another king snake slithered toward a clump of grass a few feet away. I couldn't believe my good luck and deftly pinned and captured it as well. Holding both snakes aloft, I headed back to my family, trying to avoid entangling my feet in the now frantically writhing bodies of the snakes.

My family sat at the water's edge, facing the lake and chatting happily, oblivious to the approaching danger I represented. By the time I'd made the rather difficult journey to the bottom of the slope, the snakes had managed to wrap themselves around my legs and were in the process of using that leverage to pull free of my grasp. Since snakes are essentially one long muscle with a mouth in front, they were much stronger than me and I struggled to maintain my grasp as I alerted everyone to my good fortune.

"Hey . . . *grunt* . . . everybody! Look at what . . . *gasp* . . . I found!" I yelled, attempting to stretch the snakes out, as far as a six-year-old boy could, to display their magnificent colors.

My family jumped at my announcement, especially when they realized what I held in my hands. They were mortified. But, in my young mind, I thought they were just pretending to be scared because my dad was ever the teaser.

Wow, Dad likes my snakes, I thought, watching him put on an elaborate performance, feigning absolute mind-numbing fear. The rest of the family did a wonderful job as well, screaming and carrying on. Anybody watching would have thought I'd stuck a live grenade under their collective noses. My chest swelled with pride as I joined the pretend-to-be-scared game.

I began to advance on them. "Go ahead, touch 'em," I taunted, grinning manically. "They're so smooth!" The snakes tasted the fear in the air and hissed with delight, flicking the

air menacingly with their forked red tongues. My family retreated *en masse*, teetering on the crumbling bank at the edge
of the water. Huddled together, their eyes wildly darted from
me to the snakes, and then to the grass at their feet.

There was a quick, angrily-whispered exchange in the
group. Dad was thrust forward to deal with his crazed seed.
He picked up a stick and began to circle me.

"Don't hit them!" I said, retreating a step away from Dad,
but toward the rest of the family, bringing forth a terrible, uni-
fied groan of dread from the mass of humanity now poised
behind me.

"I'm not going to hit them," Dad said, his voice stretched
and quivering an octave or two higher than normal.

I backed up a couple more steps, putting a little more distance between us. "Well, don't hit me, neither!"

"I'm not planning to hit you or them!" he said circling to
my right, focusing on the snakes.

I turned my body, keeping him in front of me. The snakes
sensed a change in the air and ceased their struggles. All eyes—
including reptilian eyes—were on the man with the stick.

"Now, what I'm gonna do," Dad said, quickly blotting the
sweat from his eyes with his sleeve, "is have you hold one snake
out at a time, and I'll use the stick to fling it into the lake."

"Nooooo!" I cried clutching both snakes to my sides.
"They'll drown!"

"No, they won't, son. Snakes can swim as good as you or me."

"I can't swim, and maybe they can't, either." I shook the
snakes' coils from my arms and bent down. "I'll just let
them go."

"No! No! Don't do that!" Dad pleaded, accompanied by confirmatory squeals from the rest of the family.

The discussion seesawed back and forth as my dad shot down each and every solution my young brain could come up with, and it was more than just a few. Finally, he convinced me that he meant the snakes no harm and this was the only way everyone, snakes included, could come out of this situation with a happy ending.

With a heavy heart, I agreed. I watched my new friends sail through the air, one at a time, and land with a small splash near the center of the lake. Dad was right after all. They could swim and quickly righted themselves and lit out for the far shore, never to be seen again.

I remember thinking, as my family lay on the ground around me, holding their hearts and gasping for breath, that I felt powerful when I was holding those snakes. People notice the guy holding the big snake, and, by God, they give him room. Can I get an "Amen," brothers and sisters?! And point me to the serpent's den—I've got some catchin' to do.

The Teenage Quest

by

Elaine Faber

I had a definite agenda. What 17-year-old girl doesn't? This is what happened.

First I had to deal with Grandma. I had reluctantly agreed to pick her up after school one Friday afternoon. She was coming to spend the weekend.

I drove into her yard. She was waiting on the porch, wearing the ugliest hat I have ever seen.

"Hi, Grandma. Nice hat."

"Well, thank you dear, I'm so glad you like it. The church had a rummage sale today. It was only a dollar."

"You sure know how to get your money's worth!" I laughed. "Are you ready to go?

We loaded Grandma's paraphernalia into my 1956 Plymouth and headed for home. Grandma chatted nonstop about the rummage sale, raspberry bushes, and moved straight on to canned pickles. I couldn't get a word in edgewise. I pretty much ignored what she was saying, anyway. I was thinking about the young man waiting for me at home. My blood ran cold when Grandma uttered the fatal words.

"Could we stop at the drug store, dear? I need to pick up a few things."

My heart sank. "Grandma, we really don't have time. It's very important that I get home early tonight."

"Now, I'll only be a minute, dear. You know I just don't get into town that often."

How do you argue with Grandma? My timetable was calculated to the minute. I had a foolproof plan. Out of school at 3:30. Pick up Grandma at 4:00, home by 5:00. Lee would have his paycheck in-hand by 5:30, and a movie date booked with me by 6 P.M.!

Lee was gorgeous—tall, dark, handsome, the current object of my affection, and Daddy's most recent carpenter's helper. I parked about a block away from the drug store, which was located between a shoe store and a massage parlor.

Grandma moved in slow motion from the car to the drug store, through the aisles and finally up to the checkout counter. That's when the real trouble started.

The clerk's register tape broke. She stopped to answer the phone and explained the entire list of sale items that week. The customer ahead of us bought an unmarked toilet brush and the clerk had to locate one with a price tag. The customer rejected the toilet brush when she heard the price.

I wrung my hands, rocking from foot to foot, watching the clock tick away the precious minutes toward 5 P.M. Finally, we reached the register to pay. Just when I saw a light at the end of the tunnel, my hopes shattered like spit on a hot griddle.

Grandma's hemorrhoid cream was marked, but the clerk had to look up the price on her enema bag. What a surprise. Grandma's total was $6.87. She licked her thumb and counted out six $1 bills. She placed two quarters, three dimes and seven pennies, one at a time, on the counter, calling the total with each added coin.

"Six dollars and 50 cents, 6 dollars and 60 cents, 70 cents, 80 cents, 81, 82 . . . "

I was ready to scream by the time she got to 87 cents.

We finally were back in the car and speeding out of town when my worst nightmare became reality. Lee lifted his hand in a casual wave as he passed our car, heading into town.

"Damn. We're too late!" I screamed. "I knew we would be late. There he goes the other way. We missed him!"

"Who did we miss, dear? And you really shouldn't say 'damn.' A lady never swears. When I get really mad, I say 'bull-dog!' It's much more ladylike!"

Grandma twisted to look over her shoulder at the cars headed the other way. I glanced in the rearview mirror and saw the rusty little foreign car, regrettably, disappearing down the road. My heart constricted. I was unable to breathe. The horrible truth pounded in my head. *I will have no date tonight!*

I gunned the engine.

"What's the matter, dear? Who was that? Should you be driving so fast? I'm getting dizzy."

I had to confess the reason for my unladylike outburst. "It was Lee, Daddy's new employee. He comes to the house every Friday night to get his paycheck then he asks me out to a movie. If I'm not there, I won't have a date!"

"Well, I'll be! Why doesn't the young man call you on the phone and ask you out?"

I shrugged. "I guess because it's payday. He knows I'll be there and he waits until Friday night to ask. Now I've missed him and he'll probably ask someone else."

The situation was bleak, but I was determined he wouldn't get away so easily. I needed a plan! The tires squealed as we rounded the corner of my street. I pulled into my driveway and skidded to a stop.

"Grandma, this is serious. No movie, no popcorn, no making out in the back seat!" *Did I say that out loud? Never mind! He's probably thinking about some other girl right this minute!*

Grandma leaned into the car, gathering her belongings, her movements somewhere between glacial time and slow motion. She picked up her sweater, her purse and her packages.

"Now where did I put that thing?" she asked, looking around. "Oh, there it is." She set her purse down and picked up the cake she had baked for dinner. The seconds ticked by. "No, that's not it." She set down the cake and picked up something else.

What could I do? He was getting away. Every second that passed, he was getting farther from my grasp.

"Get out! Get out! Get out!" I screamed, reaching for the door. "I'll bring your stuff in later!"

I slammed the door, nearly catching Grandma's fingers as she had begun to reach, once again, for the chocolate cake. Grandma's mouth dropped open.

"Well, I say!" she said, obviously annoyed by my impatience.

I slammed my trusty Plymouth in reverse, stomped on the gas pedal, spinning her tires and pitching gravel in all directions until the wheels caught the asphalt. Her engine shrieked, but almost as though she understood my teenage plight, she streaked down the road headed for town, the direction where my heart's desire had disappeared. Mercifully, there wasn't another car on the highway.

We lunged forward—60, 70, 80, 90 miles an hour. At 90 mph, her front end began to shake and rattle and the steering wheel vibrated violently in my hands. I slowed down to 85 mph.

I flipped my ponytail and slowed the car to a mere 50 mph at the city limits. Never mind the vibrating steering wheel, Lee was NOT getting away!

Several blocks ahead, traffic was stopped at the stoplight in the center of town. Lee's dilapidated little car sat immobile about nine cars back from the traffic light. The signal allowed pedestrians to cross the crosswalk then allowed one or two cars to make a left turn onto the main street and one or two cars to go either straight ahead or turn right.

The light, designed in the 1920s when Model Ts shared the street with horses and carriages, had worked in my favor. It had given me time to throw Grandma out of the car and return the mile and a half to town while Lee sat at the light, waiting to make a right turn. I thanked the long-dead City Council members who had ignored the pleas of town citizens to replace the only antiquated traffic light at the only intersection in town.

I turned right, a full block before the traffic light where the cars patiently waited. I skirted across the parking lot behind the donut shop and turned left into the alley next to the grocery store, and then swung right at the next corner. I was a good block beyond the antiquated traffic light where my intended still awaited his turn at the interminable light.

I raced several blocks ahead of the light and parked at the curb in front of the Dairy Queen, awaiting my quarry. A thin wisp of smoke rose through the cracks around my poor car's shivering hood. She had served me well.

I applied a touch of lipstick, licked my finger and moistened my eyebrows, ran a comb through my ponytail and waited the minute and a half for Lee's rusty little car to chug into view. I gloried in the sweetness of success and trembled with anticipation when he passed and glanced over at me leaning against my car at the curb. I innocently waggled several fingers in his direction. He glanced back to the road then whipped his head around, staring back over his shoulder.

He turned his car and returned to where I waited, a tantalizing smile on my innocent, hopefully alluring face. Lee passed his hand over his incredulous mouth—the mouth I planned to kiss fairly soon.

"Didn't I pass you on the highway, not 10 minutes ago, on the other side of town, headed in the opposite direction?" He pointed back toward town.

"Yes, I believe you did." I batted my beautiful brown eyes and tried to look innocent, as only a 17-year-old girl in love can look, having plotted, pursued and run her unsuspecting prey to ground.

"How could you possibly be here, on this side of town? You didn't pass me on the road." His eyes looked like a deer in the headlights. He didn't have a chance.

"I took a shortcut."

"But there's only one road through town. How did you get through the traffic light?" Up went his hands in a questioning gesture, the hands I expected to be caressing me before the night was over.

"I didn't go through the traffic light."

He ducked his head and looked into the passenger seat. "Wasn't someone else in the car?"

"That was just Grandma. I dropped her off at home before I came back into town."

Lee shook his head, wondering how I could get all the way home and back across town without passing him on the road. In truth, I had been blessed with good luck, raging hormones and an overwhelming desire to reach my objective. I had been blessed with an antiquated traffic light and armed with a hot 1956 Plymouth.

Guys really don't stand a chance. They don't understand. There are few forces in the world that can equal an adolescent female with her sights on a man. The power of a hurricane, an avalanche, a tsunami, a hurtling train or a speeding bullet doesn't hold a candle to the cunning, plotting, conniving, ruthless determination of a teenage girl in love.

I sit here today with a twinge of guilt when I think about how thoughtlessly and irresponsibly I treated my grandma that day, but to finish the story, I got my movie—and I got the guy. Grandma baked another cake and came for dinner the following Friday night. Oh, and by the way, she asked Daddy to pick her up, obviously remembering the tumultuous trip she had endured with me the week before.

Elaine got her man!
Bottom photo: Lee and
Elaine celebrate 50
years together.

Little Miss Sasquatch

by
Mary Beth Magee

Shaving your legs for the first time is a rite of passage for a girl. Since my half-Sicilian ancestry left me with Bigfoot-grade hair on my legs, I was particularly anxious to take that next step toward maturity. But Mama always said, "No" when I asked, and she always gave what she thought was a good reason.

"It'll grow back even darker and thicker!"

"Once you start, you can't ever stop!"

"European women don't shave their legs. Why should you?"

"Only tramps shave their legs before their wedding day."

"You're not old enough yet."

And my personal favorite: "Because I said so!"

I completely disagreed with her reasoning. I was 14 and feeling like the last "leg-hair virgin" on the North American continent. Dressing out for gym class was torture. Summertime and shorts season were every bit as bad. I wore black tights or stockings to hide my legs whenever I could. That solution got pretty miserable in the heat and humidity of New Orleans, but I employed it as frequently as I could and died of embarrassment when I couldn't.

Finally, after overhearing yet another wisecrack about my Black Forest legs, I decided to act. I figured that I would shave my legs on the sly, and that would be that. I mean, it wasn't like it could be glued back on once it was gone. Logically, once I shaved, I'd be set—after all, Mama had said, "Once you start, you can't ever stop." So if I went ahead and shaved my legs when no one was looking, I'd have to keep doing it. The theory sounded good to me.

Late that night, after everyone else was asleep, I slipped into the bathroom and locked the door. Quietly as I could, I took my dad's safety razor out of the medicine cabinet and climbed into the bathtub. With a trickle of water from the faucet, I wet my legs. I took a firm grip on the handle, placed the blade against my leg just above the ankle and gently pulled the razor upward along my shin.

Hmmm . . . I thought, *What was that strange thing hanging from the razor?* It was long and narrow and—that's when the pain registered! I looked down at my leg and saw a line of blood that looked about the same length as what I now realized was my missing skin attached to the razor.

The good news? I didn't scream or throw down the razor or otherwise attract attention to my predicament. But do you have any idea how hard it is to plug your mouth with just one hand while the other tries to hang on to an object that has suddenly become lethal? I tried to keep focused as I watched my blood run down the drain. *Just breathe,* I told myself, *and think this through.*

First priority—stop the bleeding. The job took a lot of toilet paper, but I was eventually successful. I flushed the bloody tissue evidence and the strip of my shin. Daddy's razor went back in its holder in the medicine cabinet, just as I'd found it.

Second priority—get to bed without starting the wound bleeding again. I hobbled as quietly as I could down the hallway to my bedroom and eased into the bed, keeping my ankle stiff so I wouldn't pull the gash open. *Made it!*

Third priority—come up with a cover story for this slash on my still-hairy leg. I cooked up what I thought was a pretty good yarn that involved a wire coat hanger left on a chair and running into the hook end of it in the dark. I even got up early in the morning and placed a coat hanger as evidence. I was feeling as though I had the whole thing worked out. I just might survive.

I am a terrible liar. I know this about myself. That is the reason I try not to tell lies. But I was going to try this time. For some strange reason (temporary insanity or divine intervention, perhaps?), my parents seemed to accept my explanation, although they gave me some funny looks for days. The cut healed in a few weeks, but the scar lasted for years. I still hated gym class and shorts season.

A year later, when the time finally came for me to shave my legs with permission, I did a much better job. Mama instructed me in the process. There was no adrenaline rush from knowing I was disobeying, I had my own non-lethal razor, I used a lighter touch and oh, yeah, this time I used shaving cream! Sadly, though, Mama did turn out to be right, and I haven't been able to stop shaving since. She told me so!

Mary Beth

A Pyrotechnicality

by
Roger Riley

Four teenage boys with nothing to do on a sweltering afternoon in the southeast Missouri Bootheel in 1966 can only mean one thing—Trouble with a capital T. We didn't have arcades, video games, VCRs or DVDs for entertainment back then.

"Let's ride to the swimmin' hole and jump in from the rope swing," suggested my friend Elmer.

"Naw. It's too hot to ride that far," countered Earl, Elmer's brother. "How about we head over to the Castor River and catch some catfish instead?"

"There's no shade. The fish'll fry before we get them off the hook," drawled my little brother Dean.

There had to be something we could do. Then my half-baked brain kicked in.

"I know. Let's try to make that homemade gunpowder again!"

How we went from swimming or fishing to making gunpowder is still one of life's mysteries to me, but four sets of eyes lit up and eight legs started scrambling. We gathered up what we thought we needed to make a batch of gunpowder. In no time at all, we were all down in Earl and Elmer's basement, or in what was more commonly known as a root cellar; it was cool, dark and small. It had an earthen floor and stairs so narrow leading down into it that only one person at a time could go up or down.

Our previous attempts had failed. That's right. A couple of us had seen an episode of *Star Trek* where Captain Kirk needed to make gunpowder, so we had tried to do this a few times already. We knew that charcoal, saltpeter and sulfur were needed and that was readily available to us country boys. After our failed attempts, we figured out that we needed a binding agent to hold the three ingredients together. As young as we were, we didn't know what that meant, but we decided it meant we needed a fourth ingredient. So out of the blue, we picked water.

First, we mixed the dry ingredients together in a tin can to make about 2 pounds of raw black powder. We then added water and mixed it up to make a murky slurry with the consistency of cake batter. We placed this mixture over a small alcohol fire to heat the mixture and evaporate the water. Once this slurry had cooked down, we ended up with a hard, dark block of something. We then hammered at the block to get it broken down into powder. We were getting more excited by the minute—it looked like the real stuff!

Now it was time to test it. Elmer, Earl, Dean and I were all pressed close to the small mound of black powder that we placed at the end of our 4-foot long workbench, far from the rest of the powdery concoction at the other end of the bench. Someone struck a match and held it to the small mound of black powder. It ignited and disappeared almost instantly with a surprisingly gentle *whoosh*. We learned that day that black powder made with the ingredients we used would burn. It also created a whole lot of smoke and that smoke smelled like rotten eggs. Lots and lots of rotten eggs.

None of that mattered to us at the time. We were all ecstatic over our success, whooping and hollering. But then, through the fog of the smoke, we simultaneously noticed that one red spark was caught in an updraft and it spiraled high toward the ceiling. We stared in amazement as the glowing ember began to fall in a downward arc toward the rest of the gunpowder we had made. At the same instant, we all realized that the little spark was about to land right in the middle of almost 2 pounds of homemade gunpowder!

Chaos reigned. It didn't take a rocket scientist to figure out that four boys crowded in a narrow access, smoky, rotten-egg-smelling root cellar with almost 2 pounds of homemade gunpowder about to explode in their midst could not possibly have a happy ending.

In one voice, shouts of "Run!" "Get outta here!" "We're dead meat!" "It's gonna blow!" and any number of expletives burst forth over the sound of the four of us frantically pushing, shoving and scrambling up the single-width staircase to escape the impending, crippling blast.

At the time, we did not know that black powder that is not packed into a container will not explode like a firecracker.

None of us were around to hear the menacing *whoosh* of the much larger detonation as the rest of our homemade gunpowder went up in smoke. By some miracle, we were all able to escape from that ready-made graveyard without any injuries. Standing on the porch in wide-eyed amazement, we watched as clouds of foul, rotten-egg-smelling smoke billowed out of the root cellar. Lucky for us, there was no fire.

The whole house smelled like rotten eggs for months after our little pyrotechnicality, and the food stored down there subsequently left an unusual aftertaste. Mister and missus were so thankful none of us were hurt that the only consequence was putting the root cellar off limits for any future experiments. To this day, none of us can figure out how the four of us got up those narrow stairs and out of that root cellar at the same time. That's one experiment I never want to try again.

Roger (above and left) and younger brother Dean

More Smart Kids— Stupid Stuff

They're at it again!

A Biker's Life

by
Dennis C. Bentley

Driving through my perfectly typical neighborhood on a perfectly typical day, I was struck by an epiphany at the sight of a little girl on a small pink bicycle, wearing a large helmet, knee pads and elbow pads—enough protective gear, in my mind, to qualify as an NHL goalie. The little bicycle, wobbling on its training wheels, was supported by a doting and protective father. Indeed, there had been an acute paradigm shift since my days as a youngster on two wheels.

We were not well off when I was very young. We had food and a roof over our heads, but the fact that my parents were struggling was no secret. I was the third of four children, which meant hand-me-downs and leftovers.

My older brother had a bicycle: a sturdy, heavy, 26-inch Western Flyer outfitted with a carrier, horn, headlight and rear reflectors. He used it almost exclusively for his newspaper route, and although I wish I could have ridden it during his off hours, it was too big for me. My sister, who always got whatever she wanted, had a Murray 20-inch girl's bike. She rarely rode it—she just wanted it. When I was about five, I tried it out. I didn't have much else to do, so I learned to ride it on my own through trial and error. Before long I had mastered balance and steering on the thing and ventured farther and farther from the front porch.

Within a few years I was spending more and more time on it, eventually graduating to Steve's abandoned, rusting Western Flyer. I left the yard, left the neighborhood and spent entire days traveling around town and its various subdivisions.

The bike would occasionally break down. Flat tires, worn bearings, loose bolts, broken axles—I learned to fix them all. I spent a lot of time at the Western Auto store looking for parts and upgrades. I eventually painted it flat black, stripped off all the chrome and stylish bits, and reduced it to bare utility. My riding apparel consisted of shorts, a T-shirt and low-rise canvas sneakers. I rode it on cracked sidewalks, skinny country roads and terrifying state highways, mile upon mile, near-miss after near-miss. Somewhere around my 13th birthday, my parents finally decided that I had earned my own bike.

Shiny red, five-speed, shifter on the bar, high rise handlebars, banana seat, tall sissy-bar, handbrakes, suspension on the seat and the front fork, a 20-inch racing slick on the back, a skinny 16-inch wheel on the front—it was a fully decked-out chopper. It was great for show, lousy for cross-country, long-distance touring. The bicycle, in its original configuration, lasted less than a year. The puny front wheel warped, the brakes failed and the finicky shifter was rendered useless.

I needed a bike—it was my only escape on long summer days. I looked over what I had and decided to construct a hybrid. I took the parts that worked from the chopper and mixed them with the sturdy frame of the Western Flyer: 20-inch rear slick, hard-chained into third gear, a rugged, 26-inch front wheel, after-market handbrakes and banana seat, low sissy-bar and high rise handlebars swept back, nearly horizontal. I kept the flat black, no chrome, no fenders, no chain guard. The brake was more cosmetic than effective and was eventually tossed.

The thing was—by today's standards—a death-trap. A well-balanced death trap. Something about that large gyroscope of a front wheel made the bike very stable. I mastered riding for miles without using my hands. I could take off from the house and make it all the way to the school, about two miles, without ever touching the handlebars. The route included a steep hill where attaining an insane velocity was possible. By the end of the summer, I was going down that hill standing on the bar, hands hovering over the handlebars.

An occasional buddy of mine had a fancier bike—it had a speedometer. He clocked me in excess of 40 miles per hour going down that hill. The bike responded perfectly, sometimes coasting for a mile or more on the brakeless, near-frictionless wheels. Slight leans turned it on curves. I went through several pairs of cheap canvas low-tops, my only means of slowing down the mechanical mutant.

Knowing that my machine was very well balanced and nearly indestructible, I also competed in suicidal figure-eight races on the school's basketball court. I found only one other person who would participate, and he had some sort of death wish, too. The rules were simple: ride as fast as you can in a figure-eight pattern. If you were unable to maintain your speed, you would crash into the other rider. Crashes were not only likely, they were expected. Like a medieval joust, the most intact survivor won. Victory was celebrated by racing down the court and jumping the ridge at the end, down 15 feet to the rutted, gravel covered parking lot. Bonus points were awarded for surviving the bone-jarring landing with testicles still intact.

My reckless, rebellious biker days came to an end one late August day as the start of my junior year in high school neared. I'd been out all day, already having navigated the subdivisions, the cemetery and through town. I was on Main Street in front of the school. Looking down the hill, I saw that the tall sprinklers on the football field were in full, sweeping, clicking spray. I saw it as a chance to cool off.

I raced down the hill—no hands—and leaned into the entrance. These were industrial sprinklers, shooting 20 or 30 feet. The first spray hit me like a wet towel, the second one like a form of water torture, the third one, well, there was no third one. Instead, a newly installed barrier between the field and the bleachers had been erected using 4-foot-tall, 4-by-4 posts strung with a single strand of aluminum clothesline. Since my glasses had been drenched, I didn't see the wire until it was too late. No brakes, my shoes worn slick from use, a sopping stretch of grass . . . it would be like trying to stop melting butter from sliding down a hot Teflon pan. I don't recall the impact.

I scraped my gasping-for-breath and aching body off the

ground. The swept-back handlebars merely guided the taut wire directly into my gut and the inside of my elbows. The bike kept going, barely slowing down for another 20 or 30 yards. I had been comically slingshotted back onto the field. I was out for a few moments; a sort of mini-shock spared me the exact details.

I was alone, as was usually the case. I crawled around, enduring non-specific pain, barely able to breathe, and found my glasses 7 or 8 feet beyond the wire. They were slightly mangled, but wearable. I walked home, most of my body numb, except for my left arm, which was stinging badly. Staggering into the kitchen, I dropped to the floor—or onto a chair—I don't exactly recall.

Mom rushed me to the local doctor who affirmed that there was no significant internal damage. Oddly, some would say miraculously, I had not broken any bones nor was I bleeding. There were bruises across my arms and belly. The doctor couldn't quite explain why I had completely lost the use of my left hand from my wrist to my fingers, but a neurologist in Nashville could. A bruised nerve. For a couple of months I had no use whatsoever of my left hand. It fell limp. I was given an aluminum brace and an Ace bandage and sported that thing well into the first semester of my junior year.

Momentarily lost in my epiphany, I snapped back to the heavily-protected, dimpled princess on the tiny, frilly pink bicycle. Times sure had changed. This little precious snowflake would probably never get to experience the nerve-sparking adrenaline rush of flying full-on down a back country road, rounding a curve and narrowly avoiding a wide farm truck. She'll never feel that other-earthly euphoria of the wheels leaving the planet behind and taking flight over a ragged, rocky ditch. She'll never balance on the bar and let go of the grips at highway speeds.

Too bad for you, cupcake. Enjoy your statistically longer, bubble-wrapped life.

Dennis

Terrified Together

by
Renee Hixson

My brother Jerry and I sat in the backyard and bemoaned our state of poverty. We were two broke teenagers with no jobs in a tiny Texas town. How were we going to survive the summer?

"Let's take out an ad," I said.

"Yeah, we'll do any job," Jerry agreed.

"No job too large or small," I responded, thinking about the wording needed for an ad in the local paper. We scraped together our change and placed the advertisement.

"No job too large, too small?" mumbled a low, tired voice over the phone a few days later. When we agreed, he said, "Pick ya up at 7 A.M."

The next morning, a horn blared from the driveway of our home. After bursting through the front door, we came face-to-face with a heavy man in stained black overalls. He was standing beside an old-model pickup filled with work material odds and ends. A large dog sat inside the cab of the pickup.

"Hop in the back of the truck," the man said, by way of introduction. "Time's a wasting!" Speechless, we did as he said.

The truck bounced and jostled down some secondary roads then turned off on a sandy back trail barely large enough for it to fit. The road wound through swampland and patches of pine groves. Finally, we came to a clearing and jumped out.

"Get busy," the man snorted, as he got out of the truck. He pointed to a pile of red bricks with cement plastered on them. "Knock the cement off these here bricks so they're good again."

The old man handed Jerry and me each a hammer then walked to a little trailer under a shade tree. Hours passed and it seemed like we had hardly done any bricks at all when the old man returned.

"Lunch," he barked. "In the trailer!"

By this time, the two of us were getting a little edgy. I followed my brother into the trailer. Surprisingly, it was cool and dark. After discreetly looking for long sharp knives, coils of rope and duct tape and finding none, I sat down in a folding chair. Jerry sat beside me. The boss grabbed the largest cast iron skillet I had ever seen and plopped it on a stove burner. Then he flung open a door next to the stove. I flinched, expecting the dead bodies of the last workers who'd been desperate enough to come and knock cement off bricks. Stunned, I stared at rows and rows of shiny unlabeled cans. *Home-canned victims?* I worried to myself.

"Every meal is a surprise," the old man said, with a smile I could barely detect through his straggly gray beard. "Unlabeled cans are cheap. Good deal."

I sure hoped that he had bought the cans at some discount place. I looked at Jerry and he looked at me. *Perhaps there was hope for us yet,* I thought.

After opening several cans, he dumped the contents into the heated skillet. Then he poured dark, thick molasses over the top. When the concoction was hot, he served us a plate-ful and we ate in silence. The sticky sweet substance was not recognized by my taste buds, but neither of us dared to make a comment.

"Time for music," our boss decided after he collected our plates. "You play the guitar?"

We both shook our heads in the negative, but a job was a job. The old man placed guitars in our laps then taught us a chord.

"Play the chord when I say," he yelled over the strumming of his own guitar. For the next little while we strummed our newly-learned chord. Finally, when the noon sun turned to af-ternoon shadows, we headed back outside.

"Bit cooler now," the old man said as he pointed to several rows of plants. "Weed the garden."

For the rest of the afternoon and into the evening, my brother and I pulled weeds. *Digging our own graves? Not!* Weeds grew only so deep, not enough for burial.

"When we going home?" Jerry whispered as the late after-noon turned to dark. It was almost impossible to see the difference between weeds and plants, and we were getting more nervous.

"It's time," the old man's gravelly voice broke through the darkness. *Time? For what? Surely, not the END! Were we ready? Could I save my brother? Could I save myself?* Before I had a chance to raise my garden hoe in defense, the old man commanded us to get into the truck.

"Time to take you kids home," he finished as he waved us out of his little garden patch. My brother and I scampered into the back of the old pickup. *Maybe this guy isn't a creature of terror. Maybe we are going home!*

Clinging to the sides of the pickup bed, Jerry and I swayed with the ruts in the road. Soon we were home. I wanted to throw myself on the ground and kiss the soil like a disaster or war survivor, but instead, I jumped down and stood by my brother. The old man climbed out of his truck. He slowly reached into his front overall pocket without saying a word. *Heaven help us!* my thoughts screamed.

The old man pulled a thick, black wallet from his pocket. He took out a wad of money and peeled off enough bills to cover the $1.75 hourly wage for each of us. Then he left, just as he came.

When he was gone, Jerry and I just looked at each other. And then we started laughing. We laughed at the sheer thought that we were alive and home, in one piece. And we even were paid for being terrified—together.

When Tommy Came Out to Play

by
Paul McDade

My dad left the United Kingdom in 1953 to find work in hopes of a better life for our family. When he finally earned enough to buy a brand new house, he brought my mother, my eight-year-old sister and me to join him. At a very young age, I found myself in a new country with a different culture and people who sounded really strange compared with Dad's heavy Scottish brogue and my mother's proper English. I was completely out of place, though I was too young to know it.

I vividly recall our next door neighbor coming over and introducing me to her daughter, who happened to be my age. She asked my mom if it would be all right for me to attend a birthday party for a boy around the corner. Mom agreed, and that's when I met my new sidekick, Tommy.

I was relieved that there were kids my age at the party who also lived in the neighborhood, but more importantly, I had my first introduction to a party with cake and ice cream. As a newcomer to the neighborhood, a foreigner with unkempt long blond curly locks and an overall squalid appearance (think of Charlie Brown's friend "Pig-Pen"), this was an opportunity for me to make friends and try to fit in.

After my first introduction to the kids at the party, I met many other kids around my age that I liked and got along with just fine . . . or so I THOUGHT! It wasn't until I started knocking on doors to see if they could come out, and being surprised when their moms came to the door instead, saying, "Not today," that I realized I wouldn't be winning the favorite-friend-of-the-year award. It took a while, but it finally became apparent to me that the neighborhood parents had become uncomfortable watching me play alongside their lovely children, evidently because I was a "wee bit" more aggressive in nature and tended to START STUFF. At the ripe old age of seven, I had already developed a reputation!

Tommy's parents, however, didn't have any restrictions that I was aware of and welcomed me as his only playmate, which, at the time, was a good thing for both of us. For his age, Tommy was a clumsy, tall, tubby kid who was always getting picked on. I befriended him, not because we were from the same pumpkin patch, but more out of necessity on my part; my reputation as a mischievous little devil now prevented me from playing with any of the other kids.

Tommy and I became pretty close friends. Even his cranky, beady-eyed old grandmother agreed to watch out—no, not BABY-sit—for us while our parents were at work and we were out of school for summer vacation. Watching over tiny tots is one thing, but having a near blind and deaf, cantankerous old granny watching over us during our nearly pre-teen years? The situation was not good for Granny, but it was great for two rambunctious boys. Tommy got an introduction to the true meaning of mischief, and was glad to partake as my co-conspirator. Who would have thought that my tubby friend would be pretty cool after all, especially since I had quickly become "the talk" of our homeowners' association? And I was particularly grateful that Granny couldn't hear well.

The best thing about hanging with Tommy was that his backyard was the woods—a kid's dream playground of trees, ponds, wildlife, huge boulders and places parents seldom ventured. The woods became the epicenter of many of the things we weren't supposed to do and would never tell our parents—unless the unforeseen happened.

We were in the woods, as usual, when we came across some matches waiting to be lit. They were talking to us. No kidding! So we climbed on top of a pile of dead trees and burrowed way down into the depths of the twisted trunks and limbs where no one could see us. We took one match at a time and positioned it between our index finger and the matchbook striker strip, shooting the matches away as they lit from the friction. This was such fun, until we saw that the leaves from within had caught on fire. In a panic, we both realized we couldn't put out the flames, so we ran to my house—two blocks away—and hid downstairs in my basement.

From a distance we could hear fire engines coming closer, and after what seemed an eternity, the telephone rang. It was Tommy's mother. We listened in horror as my mother answered, saying, "Hi, Virginia . . . Geezzz!" My mother would never have used the "queen-mother" of dirty words—the F-word—that Ralphie used in the classic *A Christmas Story*.

Right after my mom hung up, she yelled, "PAUL!" and I knew that tone! Apparently, Tommy's mother figured out who started the fire, though I'll never know how. Fortunately, she didn't tell the fire chief what she suspected.

There is an old saying about one thing leading to another. And it was another day when I received a call from Tommy who insisted that I should get on my "hi-ho" silver, banana-seat Stingray bike with gooseneck handlebars and start peddling as fast as I could, because he had a secret!

When I got to Tommy's house, his mom, dad and Granny were relaxing in the living room. Tommy led the way to his room, and with a grin, slid open his desk drawer. There they were . . . fireworks! And not the wimpy, boring sparklers, lady-fingers and cheap firecrackers that everyone had during Fourth of July, but the real darn thing! He had cherry bombs, M-80s (we called them "blockbusters") and Black Cat brand fire-crackers! I couldn't believe his dad actually bought them for him, even under the strict condition that he was to keep them out of sight and not tell his mom or Granny about them—ever.

Tommy's dad was a real nice guy, and it was easy to see that Tommy's height and size was a direct reflection of him and that he would probably be a near clone when he became an adult. I had labeled his dad a big slug. It seemed like he was always lying on the bed, fully clothed, fast asleep in the early afternoon when I came over. I had no idea that some people actually worked nights. So for him to go so far as to stick his neck out and do something mischievous behind Tommy's mom and Granny's back blew me away. Tommy's dad really had some Guts—with a capital G—and showed me that you just never knew what might happen within this seemingly *Leave it to Beaver* family!

Having said that, I couldn't believe it when Tommy looked at me, grinned and nodded, grabbed an M-80 and headed out back to do a little reconnaissance while his mother was preparing dinner! What the hell was he thinking? As Forrest Gump put it, "Stupid is as stupid does."

Tommy decided it would be a good idea to place the M-80 on the sill below their big picture window and kinda scare his family while they sat at the dining room table. For once, this was NOT my idea, and I actually entertained—for a split second—the thought of talking him out of what he was going to do. But they were his fireworks, and who was I to say what to do? Besides, I didn't get my young reputation as the talk of the neighborhood for nothing.

What I didn't know was that he had never lit off an M-80 before and had no idea what damage it could do. But I had lit one before, and what Tommy was about to do gave me a foreboding moment I obviously hadn't forgotten.

Now, mind you, Tommy was a big fella, and his mom, dad and Granny were also portly folks with relatively laid-back demeanors. I could see that this was about to change in a flash as the M-80 exploded. Instantaneously, the look on Tommy's face turned to pure horror as he watched his now quite nimble family fly from their seats. But it was music to my explosion-deafened ears that they howled simultaneously the name "THOMAS!" Yeah, "Thomas," not "PAUL!"

When the smoke drifted away, I could see that the M-80 only blew out a large chunk of the wooden window sill and knocked off the screens. To my amazement, it did not break the picture window, although the glass had violently flexed from the concussion. So much for the stash of fireworks we could have had for July Fourth—within seconds, they were GONE! We had been able to set off just one. It had been a bit like the shot heard around the world, except this wasn't Lexington and Concord—no Redcoats, but lots of red faces and two very frightened kids.

Although I've come a long way from being the mischievous little devil I was in my "Pig-Pen" days, I'll never forget the wonderful memories of shared adventures whenever Tommy came out to play.

Paul

LAKESIDE SCHOOL
1960-61

In Search of Gear

by
Beverly Higginson

The Monday after the Beatles appeared on *The Ed Sulli-van Show* in February 1964, girls in my second-period gym class couldn't stop talking about them. Not me, though. I didn't say a word. Not at first.

I had watched the show the night before and when the camera focused on Paul, I had to admit he was awfully cute. But other than that, I didn't get it. *All those screaming, crying girls. What's the big deal?* My mother watched with me, squinting at the screen, her expression a mix of pain and disbelief. "What in the world?" she muttered.

And I thought, *She's right. These girls are nuts. I would never go crazy like that. Ever. Besides, who are these guys?*

So in the locker room that morning, it was apparent the craziness in New York had traveled here to Los Angeles and infiltrated my high school. Beatles' talk was on every girl's lips.

They were asking each other, "Which one do you think is the cutest?" and "Who's your favorite?" Girls were singing in falsetto and restyling their hair to look like a Beatles' cut. In spite of Ringo's nose and John being married, girls were declaring their undying love for them. Renderings of *I Want to Hold Your Hand* wafted through the room, a cappella. Even my friend Dina grabbed my wrists—holding on like a vise grip—and wailed to the rafters, "I *love* George."

Her preference for George struck me as ludicrous. Surprised, I said, "George? Oh no. It's Paul. Paul's the one." A chorus of voices behind me chimed in: "Paul is *adorable*." Then a photo of Paul was produced and we stared at it adoringly and gushed over his left-handed guitar playing and how cool he looked in his black suit. Soon we were singing the songs, rehashing the show and mimicking John at the mike. The visual of the four of them returned to me and I actually *swooned*. How did this happen?

From indifference to devotion, I was hooked in one fell swoop.

During lunch, I caught up with my best friend Brenda. The first words out of her mouth were, "Did you see the Beatles last night?" By day's end, the two of us had succumbed completely. We declared our love for Paul. Typical—we fell for the same guy. From that moment on, everything Beatle-y consumed our lives.

But the two of us took a few digs along the way.

You see, blond-haired, blue-eyed Beatlemaniacs were a dime a dozen, and there were quite a few at my high school. And the Asian contingent, led by Dina, was well represented.

But brown-skinned Beatlemaniacs like Brenda and me were, well, scarce. We were already part of the racial minority on campus at a time when black people were still called Negroes. So in a year when Motown had coincidentally burst onto the scene, a Negro girl flipping out over the Beatles was heresy. In spite of my love for Motown, "sister" friends looked askance at the two of us as if we had a disease. They called us lame, said the music was dumb and that the Beatles had no soul.

For the briefest of moments, I wondered secretly about my sudden affinity. Did I *really* love their music? Or had I talked myself into this mania thing because basically, I was simply a dreamy-eyed, star-struck groupie at heart? Either way, idolizing the Beatles put me even further outside my group of friends, who, in a kindly sort of way, considered Brenda and me definitely not cool. And at times our behavior was unusual.

We looked enough alike to be sisters—long, dark hair, 5-feet tall, brown doe eyes—but in the four months we had known each other, we had become closer than sisters. With our intense desire to become great actresses, and how we dearly loved to emote, we played that game whenever we could get away with it. People looking at us would narrow their gaze. "You two sisters?" they'd ask, and we would smile warmly and say, "Why, yes—fraternal twins."

Friends snickered at our theatrical aspirations, but we were serious. Between the two of us, we had seen *West Side Story* five times. The dress shop scene got us into the drama club. One of our favorite things to do was dance down the sidewalk, snapping our fingers like Riff and Bernardo and leaping like ballerinas, while singing "When you're a Jet . . . " We feigned being oblivious to cars going by, but we loved it when rubberneckers got distracted. And the year 1964 was the same year Sidney Poitier won the Oscar and honestly, none of our friends seemed quite so moved as the two of us. We cheered for Sidney like he was our big brother. If he could win an Oscar, maybe we could, too.

In retrospect, becoming Beatles fanatics was inevitable. Even bold and daring.

I went Beatles crazy. In those days, a single 45 record at the local record shop cost 99 cents, and a movie magazine, a quarter. I bought any magazine with a Beatle on the cover and every record of theirs as soon as it came out. My $2-a-week allowance was practically spent before I could pry it out of my dad's hand. I baby-sat my neighbor's three-year-old to earn the $5.99 needed to buy *Meet the Beatles*, their first album. Brenda came by and we played it over and over. The music wasn't really danceable, but it was so yummy and innocent and their voices, so sweet. Just listening to Paul sing *All My Loving* brought tears to my eyes. And on the day their song *Can't Buy Me Love* came out, Brenda called and told me to turn on the radio. Deejays were playing the song every 15 minutes.

Around that same time, we discovered the fabulous *Beatles Monthly*, a British publication that advertised for pen pals. "Make a new friend, share your feelings about the Fab Four." *What an excellent idea,* I thought. *We could be goodwill ambassadors.* Within weeks of sending in our names, letters stamped *Par Avion* trickled in from across the pond. It was beyond exciting.

Then, out of the blue, when a rumor spread through school that the Beatles were leaving Saturday from LAX, I couldn't escape my own fantasy. *What if, out of the small crowd of girls waving their fond farewells, the Fab Four spotted Brenda and me? We would see them. They would see us! Our eyes would lock and . . . and . . .*

No way would we miss Saturday.

Brenda slept over the night before, but we hardly slept. We ate popcorn, we played music. We read letter after letter from the British kids, shared the photos, tried to decipher the language. Girls were *birds*, guys were *mates*, grade levels were *forms*. Nearly every boy sported a Beatles' haircut.

"I dare say," Brenda stated in a British accent, an affectation that had willfully seeped into our conversations, "What the devil does 'gear' mean? Everything is 'gear.'"

"By jove, I believe it means 'cool.'"

She held up a photo of one of the boys. "Check this one. Blimey. He's *gear*."

Looking at yet another picture of a Caucasian teen brought us back to an already-discussed subject: The Race Thing. We didn't know much about race relations in England or if their schools were integrated. We were hesitant about sending photos, especially since none of the photos sent to us were of black kids. *Would British kids be turned off because we were black? Were there black fans in England?* All we knew was the Beatles liked Chuck Berry and Little Richard. When we finally turned out the lights, we had decided to bite the bullet. We would write our letters, send our photos and let the chips fall where they may.

Early the next morning, after chucking candy bars into a bag and leaving a note that read, "Gone to an audition," we snuck out the back door and sprinted around the corner like a couple of runaway thieves.

We hustled our buns to Century Blvd, the main drag to LAX, and waited 30 minutes for a bus that never came. We had never been to the airport and didn't know how far away it was, but since getting there on foot was not the plan, desperation nudged us toward the curb. Hesitantly, and without uttering the word "hitchhike," out came our thumbs. It was literally a crossroads moment: I was facing a major something I should not do, but I was doing it anyway. My chest rose and fell in one big exhale. I felt buoyant and daring—and a little dangerous. Hitchhiking was ten times worse than ditching school or smoking in the bathroom, misdemeanors that could get me grounded or detention. But hitchhiking gone bad could be disastrous. So I'm not sure why we were smiling as we walked backward along the curb with our thumbs out, hoping someone would stop. And scared to death someone would.

So many cars drove by without even a glance that when a white pickup pulled over, our thumbs instantly dropped. My mind went blank. We looked at each other. *What do we do?* It took a moment to recall our objective. *Airport. Beatles.*

The truck waited, windows down, motor running. *It's now or never.* We eyed the driver—maybe 30—blond with a ponytail. "Where you girls goin'?" he asked, looking amused.

"LAX," Brenda said.

"We're going to see the Beatles," I added.

"Is that so?" he said, with an attitude as if he didn't believe us.

"Yeah," we responded. No hesitation. Suddenly we were tough.

He nodded. "I'm goin' that far. Hop in." He pushed open the passenger door.

I immediately understood Brenda's elbow in my rib. "Think we'll ride in back."

"Suit yourself."

As we climbed over the tailgate, Brenda said she couldn't believe we were getting into the back of some stranger's truck, and I couldn't believe it either. A flutter went through my stomach as the truck pulled into traffic. I tried not to think about how much trouble I'd be in over this stunt. That would come later—if I lived.

To calm ourselves, we sang our favorite Beatles' song— loud—rocking it as if we didn't have a care in the world.

When LAX came into view and Blondie stopped at the curb, surprise and relief caught in my throat as we jumped from the truck and waved goodbye. We rushed through the first open door not knowing what direction, what terminal, even what airline we should be looking for. We asked a ticket person.

"Gate 12," she said.

Our eyes bugged out. "Gate 12?" She pointed to her left. We took off running.

As we approached Gate 12, there was no mistaking the crush of girls in front of us, more than I had expected, most of them strangers. We spotted Dina waving frantically, and other girls from our high school. Caucasian girls, Asian girls, and now Brenda and me. We looked out at the runway, at the huge planes ready to be loaded. *Would the Beatles come through that door? Would we see them boarding?* We were all titters and giggles and nerves.

Then a hush fell over the group as a door opened and everyone stopped breathing. *Any minute they'll appear.* Brenda had a grip on my wrist. Dina's hands pressed together in prayer. No one strayed from the spot until a voice broke the silence. "Wrong terminal. They're at American!" Every girl looked at the girl next to her. *Should we go?* In a split second, like a flock of birds, we all headed for the American terminal running, running full tilt, hair flying, arms flailing.

We arrived breathless at American Airlines' terminal and discovered the tip was bogus, a diversion. Our voices rose up in a communal moan and then, pandemonium. Back and forth we all ran between terminals, in and out of doors, squealing, laughing, careening off chairs, bumping into walls and each other. Brenda was ahead of me then behind me, doubled over in laughter. I thought of those screaming girls on television. We were them. No clear direction, but surging ahead anyway. All of it in desperate pursuit of four British singers who quite possibly had boarded a plane earlier and were on their way to parts unknown.

A voice came over the loudspeaker, announcing that if we didn't have a ticket, to go home. Nobody moved. We played dumb. *Were they speaking to us?* Sniffles could be heard, because some girls were now crying. But no one moved until the message was repeated. Chants of "Yeah, yeah, yeah" went up— our last hurrah. Later, in twos and threes, disappointed girls, including us, straggled out of the terminal.

Once we were outside, Brenda and I caught up with Dina. Her jaw dropped when we told her we had hitchhiked to the airport. "So cool," she said, adding she would never have had the nerve. Her mom was picking her up, so we gladly accepted her offer of a ride home. I mentioned it was weird Dina's mother playing chauffer, and ours not knowing where we were. It struck a nerve. The three of us sank to the curb laughing. It took the edge off our disappointment.

On the ride home, we offered confessions. Brenda said she stopped believing at Gate 12 because it seemed impossible. I stopped believing at the American terminal and gave up my fantasy. Only Dina had kept the faith to the bitter end that we would actually see the Fab Four.

We never got to the bottom of the original rumor, but we figured the Beatles probably weren't even there that day. Still, for a few hours, a bunch of strangers turned into lunatic sisters on a crazy mission. Nothing beyond that mattered.

It was all gear.

Beverly

Do You Want Fries with That?

by
Christine Cacciatore

The illusion is shattered, if it ever even existed. The illusion that my children should have of me as the perfect mother is gone. During breakfast at a restaurant last December, my mother chose to share with my children one of the more embarrassing stories of my childhood—no, wait, *the* most embarrassing story—over our eggs, ham and pancakes.

This moment conveys one event in a long line of humiliating things that have happened to me. I was about 12. Some of you may remember that McDonald's had come out with a contest to win a Big Mac T-shirt. To win the contest, you simply had to harness the courage to stride right up to the counter and sing the famous "Two All-beef Patties" jingle under a certain time limit. That was it.

How simple! Even I could do that! I had practiced and practiced and had polished my Big Mac song to a competitive time. I was ready. That T-shirt was all but mine. I just knew in my heart that they surely had never heard anyone sing it faster. I would probably be asked to do a commercial. Everyone would know of my special talent.

Finally, my long-suffering mother took me to our local McDonald's so I could attempt the feat. Entering the restaurant, I lost a little bit of my nerve, but my mother nudged me up to the counter and before I knew it, and more importantly before I lost my courage, I was at the counter loudly belting out my record-shattering speedy version of the Big Mac song to the gum-smacking, bored-looking cashier behind the counter. She stood there with her head cocked, letting me sing it out. When I was done, I looked at her, hoping that I sung it under the time limit.

"That contest ended a week ago," she said—snarkily I might add. "Can I take your order? Let me guess. You want a Big Mac?"

Time stood still.

There would be no T-shirt. No free Big Mac. No commercial. I had just sung a song in front of not only the entire amused McDonald's crew, but also several hungry customers who were studiously avoiding any eye contact with me. And it seemed to me that the employees got a little more industrious with their napkin-filling and ice machine replenishment.

It was over. I had sung a song that would win me not a T-shirt, but years of humiliation with a large side order of embarrassment.

However, something good did come out of that debacle at Mickey D's almost 33 years ago. There we were, the day after a wonderful Christmas—which happened to be my daughter's 21st birthday—sitting in the restaurant as a family and laughing our fool heads off, all over my mother sharing my most stupid-kid stunt, ever. The moment was priceless.

I wish I could go back in time to that 12-year-old version of myself and let her know that the embarrassment would wear off, she'd get better T-shirts than the Big Mac T-shirt she tried so hard to win, her barely-breathing social life would recover from that catastrophe, and she'd eventually be able to go back into a McDonald's without needing a Xanax.

I would also tell her to avoid ordering a certain fish sandwich at the Burger King on the other side of town, but we'll save that story for another day.

Bully for Who?

by
Sheila Hudson

As an only child growing up in suburban Atlanta in the late 1950s and early 1960s, I loved visiting my cousin in northern Georgia. Linda lived on a farm and was my best friend. She was the sister I never had.

The summer Linda turned 16, I was still 15. She was allowed to date, but I—not having reached that magical age—would have to wait until December. That seemed eons away, so we dreamed up a way to double date. After everyone was asleep, we'd sneak out of the house and meet two local boys Linda knew. Later, we'd sneak back in. It was a great plan!

We congratulated ourselves on our ingenuity. On the appointed night, we retired early, which should have been an immediate tip-off to Aunt Mary Nell. Wearing good clothes under our nightgowns, we lay sweating on the iron poster beds until Mama Sewell and Aunt Mary Nell were sound asleep.

At her signal, I raised Linda's bedroom window for her to climb through. She tore her new capris and let out a swear word, but fortunately, Aunt Mary Nell's rhythmic snoring assured us that all was still well. We sneaked to the gate separating the property from an adjoining farm owned by our Uncle Roy and Aunt Margaret. Linda lifted the gate latch and stepped through.

Swatting at an insect circling my head, I let the gate slam against the fence post with a thunderous crash, which startled us both. We strained our eyes against the darkness and were relieved to see that no house lights came on. We thought we were in the clear when suddenly, we heard a rumbling in the bushes. Someone, or something, brushed past us. Something very large with wiry hair and hot breath!

Then the awful truth hit. "Oh, no! Horatio is out!" gasped Linda. "We've got to put him back."

We chased Uncle Roy's prize bull in the moonlight. Linda yelled, "Catch his head! Hold him!" But there was no way I—a city girl—was going to grab that bull's head. As we ran, we prayed. Uncle Roy would never forgive us if anything happened to Horatio—he was the best bull in the county.

Finally realizing we'd never catch him, Linda suggested we call Aunt Margaret. "She'll help us corral him, and she won't squeal either. Aunt Margaret's a pal."

"No," I protested. "We can't tell anyone. My dad will kill me if he gets wind of this. I'll never be able to visit you again."

We exchanged breathless protests until finally we agreed for Linda to sneak back inside and telephone Aunt Margaret. Luckily, Aunt Margaret was still up and alone. When she arrived, she left her truck lights on, pointing them in our general direction. Cautiously, she approached Horatio.

Suddenly, Horatio bolted and she grabbed his tail as he went by! Aunt Margaret isn't a small woman, but that old bull dragged her around the yard like a rag doll. She was screaming at the top of her lungs, so all the house lights quickly came on.

We were in for it now! I figured my folks would come for me first thing in the morning. I might as well just start packing. Meanwhile, Aunt Margaret's ride continued through briars and bushes, across plowed fields and over the lawn. Her firm grip held. Then, unexpectedly, Uncle Roy showed up carrying a little silver whistle. He blew it, and Horatio stopped dead in his tracks. He lowered his massive head and trotted up to Uncle Roy like a pet retriever.

After prying Aunt Margaret's 10-finger death grip off Horatio's tail, Uncle Roy led him back through the gate and into the barn. We helped Aunt Margaret inside, picking twigs and beggar's lice off her clothes. While Mama Sewell got her a glass of water, we managed to deposit her in the recliner. Obviously, we never made it to our date rendezvous point.

Incredibly, my parents never found out about this episode. The question of how Linda and I happened to be outside was never raised. Everyone assumed we'd heard Horatio rumbling around and tried to put him up ourselves. They never questioned why we were wearing our good clothes.

For days afterward, we giggled at how funny Aunt Margaret looked holding onto Horatio's tail. We also marveled at Horatio's obedience to Uncle Roy's whistle. Forty years later, Linda and I laugh about our double date with Horatio T. Bull-by.

We Trust You

by
Brent Goldstein

Every fall at every high school across America, there is at least one dumbass senior who decides to throw a *small* party to kick off his/her glorious senior year. Usually this decision corresponds with an even dumber decision by said senior's trusting parents to leave him/her alone at home for the weekend. In September 1984, I was that dumbass senior.

I don't remember their exact words when my parents left, but I'm sure it wasn't too far off from Tom Cruise's movie dad in *Risky Business*: "Joel, as far as the house is concerned, just use your best judgment. We trust you." While my name wasn't Joel and I didn't dance around in my underwear playing air-guitar to Bob Seger, I did make the requisite phone calls to several friends to let them know that the foxes had left the henhouse. It was party time: kegger at Brent's house Saturday night after the football game!

We had a social committee consisting of me and six others (names withheld to protect the idiots). Two guys took care of the kegs by traveling down to Washington, D.C. where the drinking age was 18. Two guys took care of cups, ice and other supplies. The rest of us spread the mojo and hooked up the stereo. We figured we'd have maybe 50 to 75 people and that two kegs of cheap beer would suffice. We would charge $3 for girls and $5 for guys and just knew we'd come out of this with a nice profit to cover—what else—beer money for the next few months!

The party started at 6 P.M. on a beautiful early September, Saturday evening. By 7 P.M., 75 "friends" had shown up. By 8 P.M., my backyard was packed and we were halfway through the second keg. By 9 P.M., we numbered well over 150 hormonal teens, and we were pretty much OUT OF BEER! We thought of sending some guys back downtown to buy more kegs, but none of us were in any condition to drive and the round trip would take at least an hour. The masses were getting unruly. The liquor cabinet was raided, but I had clairvoyantly relocated the contents to a safe place before the party started. At 9:15, two neighbors showed up at my front door complaining about all the cars and noise. To make matters worse, word filtered in from my rear flank that two freshman girls were so hammered that they could barely walk or speak. One had actually fallen over the back fence into the field behind my house!

The party had become a full-fledged, Code-Red nightmare and I needed to get all the sloshed teenagers off my property NOW! I quickly determined that making a loud announcement saying, "Pretty please—leave!" might result in an ass-kicking (my own) followed by rampant vandalism. So I did the next best thing. I snuck into a quiet room and secretly called the police, begging them to come to my house and break up the party. I then gathered my composure, calmly walked out back, found the largest guy I could and told him in my very best faked-panicky voice, "My f_ _king neighbors called the f_ _king cops and they'll be here in 10 f_ _king minutes!"

It worked. He freaked. Within minutes, communal fear of the impending hammer of Johnny Law led to rapid crowd dispersal and a very blessed exit. The empty kegs were quickly transported to an awaiting car's trunk, the two drunken harlots were escorted to safety, and all cars within 500 yards of my house disappeared. By the time the police arrived, there was no incriminating evidence beyond a few remaining party goers filtering out. This was an important point as I needed at least a few people to be able to recount visual confirmation of police arrival to save face come Monday.

Fortunately, there was minimal damage and mess. My buddies and I grossed about $1,000, which covered the $100 for beer and supplies and another $100 for an emergency cleaning service. My parents did learn of the party, but the details were so fuzzy and whitewashed that I got off with a slap on the wrist. My punishment was mitigated by good reports from the neighbors regarding how we responsibly scoured the streets and picked up trash in the hours after the party.

So what did I learn from this? Well, for one, this was my first valuable real-life lesson in the study of risk versus reward. While an $800 profit was a lot of money for some snot-nosed teens, I quickly realized that the money wasn't worth the stress and risk. Secondly, the whole experience gave me insights on crisis management and staying calm in the face of mayhem.

And while both of these lessons have served me well in my adult life, there was one even more very important lesson I learned: I will never, EVER, leave *my* kids home alone!

Brent

NYMB Series Founders

Together, Dahlynn and Ken McKowen have 60-plus years of professional writing, editing, publication, marketing and public relations experience. Full-time authors and travel writers, the two have such a large body of freelance work that when they reached more than 2,000 articles, stories and photographs published, they stopped counting. And the McKowens are well respected ghostwriters, having worked with CEOs and founders of some of the nation's biggest companies. They have even ghostwritten for a former U.S. president and a few California governors and elected officials.

From 1999 to 2009, Ken and Dahlynn were consultants and coauthors for *Chicken Soup for the Soul*, where they collaborated with series founders Jack Canfield and Mark Victor Hansen on several books such as *Chicken Soup for the Entrepreneur's Soul; Chicken Soup for the Soul in Menopause; Chicken Soup for the Fisherman's Soul;* and *Chicken Soup for the Soul: Celebrating Brothers and Sisters*. They also edited and ghost-created many more Chicken titles during their tenure, with Dahlynn reading more than 100,000 story submissions.

For highly acclaimed outdoor publisher Wilderness Press, the McKowen's books include national award-winner *Best of California's Missions, Mansions and Museums; Best of Oregon and Washington's Mansions, Museums and More;* and *The Wine-Oh! Guide to California's Sierra Foothills.*

Under Publishing Syndicate, the couple authored and published *Wine Wherever: In California's Mid-Coast & Inland Region*, and are actively researching wineries for *Wine Wherever: In California's Paso Robles Region*, the second book in the Wine Wherever series.

If that's not enough, the McKowens are also the creators of the Wine Wherever iPhone mobile winery-destination journaling app and are currently creating a travel television show under the same brand (www.WineWherever.com).

Ken and Dahlynn in Ho Chi Minh Square in Hanoi, Vietnam.

NYMB Co-Creator

About Laurel (Bernier) McHargue

Laurel was born and raised in Braintree, Massachusetts by Patricia (Malone) and Charles Murray Bernier. The fourth of five daughters, Laurel always knew her path would be different from her siblings' and would take her far away from her suburban home.

After graduating from Braintree High School in 1977, she attended Smith College, despite warnings from her guidance counselor she probably wouldn't be accepted. Laurel completed three successful semesters before deciding she was bored. Never having been a Girl Scout or having done anything truly difficult in her life, she applied for admission, and was accepted, to the United States Military Academy at West Point, New York. Laurel started from scratch as a lowly "plebe" and graduated proudly four years later in 1983, which was the fourth graduating class in the school's storied history to include women.

One month later, as an Army Second Lieutenant, Laurel married her most extraordinary classmate Mike McHargue and continued to serve for nine years active duty in the Army followed by three years in the Reserves. During those years, Laurel earned her M.A. in English and the couple welcomed two remarkable and brilliant sons, Nick and Jake, to their family. Her young boys transitioned her to civilian life and kept her busy in the many homes they lived in, moving from place to place until

Mike retired from the Army in 2003.

After volunteering for years and coaching Odyssey of the Mind and Destination Imagination teams in her boys' schools while they were young, Laurel earned her teaching certificate while trying desperately to teach English to seventh graders in a doomed middle school. When the school closed in 2007, the family moved to Leadville, Colorado where she taught high school English for four years.

In 2011, Laurel decided it was time for another big challenge. With both sons off to college, she resigned from her teaching job, emptied out and converted her youngest son's room into an office, and declared herself a professional writer, something that had been on her bucket list for as long as she could remember.

Laurel is currently an adjunct English instructor at Colorado Mountain College in Leadville and has been working with Publishing Syndicate since March of 2012. She is the co-creator of this title and *Not Your Mother's Book . . . On Dating*. You can find her writings and short stories in other NYMB titles, in *Colorado Central Magazine* and on her blog at www.leadvillelaurel.com.

Laurel

Contributor Bios

Marilyn Acker is a freelance writer of nonfiction stories. Her current project is a travelogue book about backpacking with her daughter across Costa Rica and Mexico. She is a member of Carteret Writers Group of North Carolina and Seascribes Critique Group. Marilyn resides and writes at Emerald Isle Beach, North Carolina.

Diana M. Amadeo is an award-winning author whose work can be seen in books, e-books, newspapers, magazines and online. She can be reached at da.author@comcast.net. Visit her website at http://home.comcast.net/~da.author/site/

Jerry W. Baker is a native Texan. He resides with wife Kathy and three pooches: Hank, Samantha and Abby. His alma mater is Texas Tech University. After college, Jerry proudly served in the U.S. Marine Corps before starting a lifelong career in the life insurance industry.

Kathleene S. Baker resides in Plano, Texas, with husband Jerry and three fur kids: Hank, Samantha and Abby. She is a co-creator of *Not Your Mother's Book...On Dogs*, as well as a freelance writer, contributing to many publications, and an author of a weekly, monthly and quarterly column. www.txyellowrose.com

Francine Baldwin-Billingslea is a mother, grandmother, breast cancer survivor and a second-time-around newlywed who has recently found a passion for writing. She has been published in over 21 anthologies, several magazines and online. Francine loves traveling, writing and spending quality time with her loved ones.

Banjo Bandolas' stories have appeared in local, national and international publications. His style of storytelling reflects his southern roots. Previous anthologies include *Dead on Demand; Chicken Soup for the Fisherman's Soul; Ghosts from the Coast;* and *Chicken Soup for the Soul Healthy Living* series. He works as a globe-trotting beer writer for Realbeer.com.

Dennis C. Bentley is an IT consultant in suburban St. Louis. He lives in rural Jefferson County with his infinitely patient wife Angel, who is a dog trainer and rescue shelter volunteer. His essays have been published in *My Dog is My Hero* and *My Teacher is My Hero*. www.dcbentley.com

Ireta Black will turn 90 years old in January 2013. This story marks her first time as a published author. Ireta is active in her retirement community and church and loves any and all new adventures that come her way. But what she loves most is hearing from her pre-teen grandson David!

Ann Marie Brick retired from the practice of law in 2009 and moved from Des Moines, Iowa to Leadville, Colorado the same year. She is always training for the Leadville 100 Mile Race, but never makes it more than half way. Ann Marie loves living at the 10,200-foot elevation!

Carol Brosowske is a native Texan and lives in Plano, a suburb of Dallas. She married Jim in 1974 and is the mother of three grown children. She has three dogs and would love more, if Jim would only agree. Her hobbies include quilting, cross-stitch, decorating and, of course, writing.

Maureen Bureson, now retired, is reflecting on her interesting and unusual life while contemplating writing a memoir. She was honored with a second place award in the Creative Writing Competition sponsored by the Albert Anthony Foundation for Cultural Arts, Grants & Scholarships. Maureen lives in Arizona.

James Butler spent his first 12 years learning about life on a small Midwest family dairy farm. The time, while short, cemented values, experiences and memories that have lasted over 50 years and counting. Though it was a hard life, he said he would not trade those years for any others. Learn more at www.Facebook.com/RaptorRavine.

Christine Cacciatore is married to a wonderful man, has three great kids and one ridiculous dog. They reside in the Midwest where she blogs at *The Life and Times of Poopwa Foley*. Christine is also working on a collection of funny stories sure to embarrass her family and delight her fans.

Kathe Campbell lives on a Montana mountain with her donkeys, kitties and a Keeshond. Three children, 11 grands and three greats round out her herd. She is a prolific writer on Alzheimer's and contributing author to the *Chicken Soup for the Soul* series, *RX for Writers*, magazines and medical journals.

Dawn Keeley Caunce is a United Kingdom-based writer. A busy mum of three, she is currently freelancing articles and short stories while making sure, in her position as a moderator, the writing forum she belongs to is a happy place for members. Dawn is currently working on a range of children's picture books.

Robert Drummond is a retired aquatic biologist who now enjoys writing poems (mostly Haiku) and short, true-life stories. He currently lives in Montrose, Colorado along with his wife Bonnie.

Terri Duncan, a high school administrator, is a devoted wife and mother of two grown children. She hopes they support her in her retirement so she can pursue her dream of writing. Terri has authored numerous short stories and a book for young readers—*Camping Reservations: Body of Lies.*

Terri Elders lives near Colville, Washington, with two dogs and three cats. A lifelong writer and editor, her stories have appeared in dozens of periodicals and anthologies. She is a co-creator for the NYMB series. She blogs at atouchoftarragon.blogspot.com. Terri is a public member of the Washington State Medical Quality Assurance Commission.

Elaine Faber is a member of California Writers Club, Sisters in Crime, Inspire Christian Writers, and an editor on the 2012 *Inspire Faith Anthology.* Her stories are printed in magazines and anthologies. Elaine lives in Elk Grove, California with her husband, Lee. They celebrated their 50th wedding anniversary in June 2012.

Carole Fowkes has had a number of articles and stories appear in various anthologies. She is also the author of six books published by Ink Lion Books. She currently lives in Texas and has a great relationship with her sister, who is still in Ohio.

Pamela Frost lives in Medina, Ohio. Her award-winning book *Houses of Cards* (available on Amazon and Kindle) is the story of a family who tried getting rich in real estate and their hilarious misadventures. She is co-creator of two upcoming *Not Your Mother's Books: RV Adventures* and *On Do-It-Yourselfers.*

Brent Goldstein is an investment advisor, occasional lawyer, sometimes freelance writer and as-often-as-possible recreational enthusiast. He has been published (not so) extensively on his personal blog (www.skibrent.blogspot.com) and has spent the last 20 years struggling to come up with a decent story for his first novel.

Betty Guenette has written numerous award-winning short stories and been published online and in magazines, newspapers and anthologies. She is currently working on a mystery series. Betty is a member of the Sudbury Writers' Guild and the Canadian Authors Association.

Lisa Hemrich lives with her husband Steve and their two children Tyler and Kaitlyn in southern Illinois. She teaches English and sponsors the school newspaper and yearbook at Flora High School.

Beverly Higginson, a theater arts major in college, was born in Vancouver, British Columbia. Her first query letter resulted in publication with a byline in a national magazine, followed by three years of writer's block. Happily writing again, she resides in Eagle Rock, California with husband Howard and Blue, the cat.

Renee Hixson is a mom, a writer and a willing participant in the greatest adventure ever—figuring out her purpose on planet Earth. She believes in God, questions everything and is not surprised by any strange turn of events. Her blog, should you dare to peek, is www.livinginloserville.com.

Sheila Hudson is published in *Chocolate for Women, Chicken Soup for the Soul,* and the *Patchwork Path* series and a number of magazines and newspapers. She is a columnist for *Purple Pros; Southern Writer,* and *Costumer Magazine,* and past president and co-president of the Southeastern Writers Association. sheilahudson.writer@gmail.com; www.sheilashudson.com

Kevin Kane resides in Rockville, Maryland with his wife Jill, three daughters, and faithful canine, Dog Julio de Rosemont Kane. Kevin marches to his own beat, usually iambic pentameter. He is a recovering attorney and very amateur mountain-bike racer.

Gregory Lamping is a psychiatric nurse living in Kirkwood, Missouri.

John J. Lesjack, a graduate of both St. Veronica School and East Detroit High School, is now a retired grade school teacher living in Santa Rosa, California. Responses may be sent to Jlesjack@gmail.com.

Rebecca MacKenzie writes from her home in Oconomowoc, Wisconsin. Her work appears in teaching, writing, parenting and religious publications. A prize-winning essayist, Rebecca also is a poet published in a national anthology. She is an early childhood educator who enjoys developing curriculum. Foremost, however, Rebecca is a wife and mother.

Mary Beth Magee, a New Orleans native, somehow survived a stupid kid childhood. She's been writing as long as she can remember. Her subjects include news and feature articles for print and online publications, book and movie reviews, short fiction and poetry.

Glady Martin lives in a small hamlet in British Columbia, Canada, where she enjoys sharing her stories through words. Having written since grade school, she says, "Writing is a way of breathing for me . . . it is a wonderful tool for expressing myself." Glady also enjoys writing poetry.

Carole Spearin McCauley has written 12 commercially published books—medical nonfiction, literary and other novels. Her mysteries—*Cold Steal* and *A Winning Death*—appear from Hilliard & Harris. Her love/business/arson novel *How She Saved Her Life* appears soon from She Writes Press. Her short work, including prize-winning pieces, appear widely.

Paul McDade was born in England, came to Braintree, Massachusetts, at age 3, married his hometown sweetheart in 1977, commissioned as a Marine Corps officer, and currently works in Houston. Paul enjoys writing stories about special lifetime moments and looks forward to sharing quality time with those who enjoy his tales.

Jamie Miller grew up in Wyoming, entering the exciting/embarrassing world of high school in 1950. Surviving that, he studied engineering, then worked 37 years at NASA. Typical engineer, he wrote so poorly he began writing as a challenge. He's improving. His wife, son and two daughters are all competent writers.

Pat Nelson, writer and editor, is co-creator of two *Not Your Mother's Books: On Parenting* and *On Grandparenting*. She has written newspaper columns, contributed to *Chicken Soup for the Soul*, written one book, *You . . . The Credit Union Member* and is currently writing a nonfiction book about a tuberculosis sanatorium.

Elsilee Patterson comes from a large family of educators. After 35 years of teaching, she retired from her beloved career in 2003 and started writing. She believes every person is a teacher, and she's learned countless valuable lessons from many, including Mr. Loptien, her caring teacher in her story "First Chair."

Anola Pickett is a retired teacher and school librarian. She is the oldest of six children and has lived in Kansas City, Missouri for most of her life.

Joyce Rapier, lifelong resident of Van Buren, Arkansas is a published author of several books and has inclusions in *Chicken Soup for the Soul* and the *Literary Cottage*. She writes a weekly column "Do You Remember" for the *Press Argus-Courier* in Van Buren.

John Reas is a former engineer and Army officer who has had a lifelong ambition to become a writer. This is his second story in the *Not Your Mother's Book* series and he looks forward to continuing to develop his passion for writing.

Dana Reynolds received her bachelor of science in mathematics, her masters in inclusive education, and is adjunct faculty at Westmoreland County Community College in Pennsylvania. She is the mother of two brilliant and hilarious young adults and two rescued cats.

Roger Riley grew up in America's heartland. Country living and enjoyment of the simple pleasures of life in a time before television, radio, and technology were readily available in his small town, made him an avid fan of all genres. Writing has always been entertainment and a creative outlet for him.

Kendall Roderick was sheltered as a kid, not being able to watch PG-13 movies until she was 16. The lack of common knowledge actually helped in the long run and resulted in an undisturbed fairytale mind. As a child, she started writing and hasn't stopped.

Kristen Shalosky is still a stupid kid, but just a little bigger. When she's not making her mother's hair gray, she enjoys playing rugby and exploring the mountains in her new home state—Colorado.

Phil Silver was born in 1946 in Jacksonville, Florida and raised in Burbank, California. With a teaching credential from U.C. Berkeley, he taught adult and special education classes. He was an on-air personality at KNGS in Hanford, California and worked 23 years at Pacific Bell before becoming an award-winning author.

Bobby Barbara Smith is known widely for her short stories and poetry published in *Memories & Motherhood* and *Faith Writers Speak,* as well as online. She enjoys gardening, singing and performing with various musicians. Bobby currently resides in North Central Arkansas with her husband and two fur babies. indy113@yahoo.com

Susan Sundwall freelances and writes mysteries from her home in upstate New York. Her first mystery, *The Red Shoelace Killer—A Minnie Markwood Mystery*, will be available November 1, 2012 on Amazon or from the publisher Mainly Murder Press. Visit her blog at www.susansundwall.blogspot.com

Randy Svisdahl has lived and worked in the forests of British Columbia all his life. Currently, he resides in Holberg, British Columbia with his wife Janet and their two Airedales—Dutch and Doc. Aching for the beautiful wilderness of the Bella Coola Valley, Randy and Janet try to get back to the valley they still call home whenever they can.

Annmarie B. Tait lives in Conshohocken, Pennsylvania, with her husband Joe Beck where she enjoys cooking and many other crafts. She has contributed to several volumes of *Chicken Soup for the Soul, Reminisce Magazine* and other anthologies. She is also a recent nominee for the annual Pushcart Prize literary award. Email: irishbloom@aol.com

Anna Roberts Wells was born and raised in central Arkansas, attended Hendrix College and taught English one year, and then went on to become a social worker with foster children. Now retired, she writes, volunteers and enjoys a family consisting of a husband, four grown children and four grandchildren.

Story Permissions

Publishing Syndicate

Publishing Syndicate LLC is an independent book publisher based in Northern California. The company has been in business for more than a decade, mainly providing writing, ghostwriting and editing services for major publishers. In 2011, Publishing Syndicate took the next step and expanded into a full-service publishing house.

The company is owned by married couple Dahlynn and Ken McKowen. Dahlynn is the CEO and publisher, and Ken serves as president and managing editor.

Publishing Syndicate's mission is to help writers and authors realize personal success in the publishing industry, and, at the same time, provide an entertaining reading experience for its customers. From hands-on book consultation and their very popular and free monthly *Wow Principles* publishing tips e-newsletter to forging book deals with both new and experienced authors and launching three new anthology series, Publishing Syndicate has created a powerful and enriching environment for those who want to share their writing with the world. (www.PublishingSyndicate.com)

NYMB Needs Your Stories!

We are looking for hip, fun, modern and very-much-today type stories, just like those in this book, for 30 new titles in the NYMB series. Published contributors are compensated.

Submission guidelines at www.PublishingSyndicate.com

More *NYMB* Titles

Look for new
Not Your Mother's Books
coming soon!